The Allen Family

of Amherst County, Virginia

CIVIL WAR LETTERS

First Edition
Limited to One Thousand Copies

No. _____

Charles W. Turner, Editor

April 1995

The Allen Family
of Amherst County, Virginia
CIVIL WAR LETTERS

Charles W. Turner, Editor

Rockbridge Publishing Company
Berryville, Virginia

Published by

Rockbridge Publishing Company
P.O. Box 351
Berryville, VA 22611
(703) 955-3980

Library of Congress Cataloging-in-Publication Data

The Allen family of Amherst County, Virginia : Civil War letters /
    Charles W. Turner, editor. — 1st ed.
        p.   cm.
    Includes index.
    ISBN 1-883522-06-4
    1. United States—History—Civil War, 1861-1865—Personal
narratives. Confederate. 2. Allen family—Correspondence.
3. Amherst County (Va.)—Biography. 4. Soldiers—Virginia—
Amherst County—Correspondence. 5. Confederate States of
America. Army of Northern Virginia. 6. Virginia—History—Civil
War, 1861-1865—Campaigns. 7. United States—History—Civil
War, 1861-1865—Campaigns. I. Turner, Charles Wilson.
E605.A555   1995
973.7'82—dc20   95-13073
                                                          CIP

10 9 8 7 6 5 4 3 2 1
First Edition

Table of Contents

Dedication

This book is dedicated to Mrs. Stella Allen for her efforts to preserve the history of the Allen Family and home.

Preface

The Allen Family of Amherst County in the Civil War consists of a set of letters which six brothers wrote to their Mother and Sisters during the war. They show the fears, the loves, the hopes and battles of the period. These letters were sent to me by Mrs. Stella Allen, whose husband was a son of one of the letter writers. Mrs. Allen now (1994) lives in the Odd Fellows Nursing Home in Lynchburg, Virginia. My friends, Cora B. and Florence Womeldorf of East Lexington, Virginia, cousins to the Allens, sent the letters to me.

This book reveals what one family had to undertake in the War efforts. The boys entered the service at different times. Each continued to live at home and take care of the mother. They hoped the youngest would never have to enter the service. He fooled them and entered the service in the last year of the War. They fought in Virginia almost exclusively. Half of them had stays in a Confederate hospital, which they describe very well. Two of them gave their lives in the service.

Mrs. Allen has written in longhand the story of the old Allen home, which was valuable to this work. Many of the letters were lost, but those saved tell an interesting story. The original letters are in the Special Collections of the Washington & Lee University Library.

Special appreciation is expressed to the persons above. Also to Katherine Tennery, the publisher, and Mrs. Margaret Letrude of Lexington, Virginia, who typed the original copy.

Charles W. Turner
November 20, 1993

Introduction

Thomas Oliver and Mary Garnette Tinsley Allen moved to Amherst County, Virginia, from Big Four, Tennessee, in 1827. The family arrived in a covered wagon and settled on a farm they purchased from a Mrs. Dodd. One of the fields on the 181-acre farm is still, in 1994, called the Dodd Field.

The wagon carried them over the turnpike that ran almost parallel to the south branch of the Buffalo River, which runs through the place. At that time, the river and road ran in front of the large (eight-room) wooden house with its log kitchen behind. Food was carried from the kitchen to the dining room through a whistling tunnel, although the Allens never had slaves in Virginia. One slave in Kentucky, named Mary, had gotten into the wagon to come east, but Thomas refused to bring her.

Thomas and Mary had ten children, six sons: Thomas Oliver II, Tinsley Linsley, Richard Harrison, James Henry, and Devereaux Frederick; and four daughters: Mary Jane Allen Whitten, Elizabeth (Eliza) Allen Clements , Sallie and Ellen. When the war began, Thomas, Mary and Eliza were married and living away from the Allen home farm.

All of the boys joined the Confederate service.

A small collection of their letters, written to their widowed mother and sisters and to one another, have survived. The letters are filled with the misspellings, lack of punctuation and paragraphing found in many letters of the period. On the assumption that the reader of these letters is interested more in their content and spirit than their style, spelling and punctuation have been edited. The following is a true copy of part of one of William's letters for comparison.

Dear Ma and Sisters I Seat my self this night to drop you all a few lines to inform you all of my helth &c I am quite well at present Hoping when these few lines come to hand tha may find you all well and enjoying your Selves as well as usual Dear Ma wee landed to Staunton Tuesday night after leeving home and wee landed to Winchester the 9 and wee stayed their all night and Reported and tha Returned us back to Front Royal and wee found them Near Seaders Ville [Cedarsville] a bout 12 Miles from wh Winchester wee traveled at Least 2 hundred Miles Before wee landed to our Reg wee traveled 2 days in snow which was as disagreeable weather as I ever traveled Which I Landed to my company the 11 Nov and my company was verry glad to see me I am verry well sadisfied with my capt he lows us as meny privolidges as I could ask him he has lowed us to Forrowging wich every day I can Leave camp wee make from 5 to 10 dollars Ma if wee could meet with eny thing to sell wee could do well I has Traveled a bout 12 to day and I came across 1 Bushel of apples I paid 5 dollars for them and sold them for 14 dollars ...

This photograph and the one below show the Allen Farm as it looked in 1990.

The Allen Farm prior to 1970.

Mary Jane Allen Whitten was a sister to
the Allen boys who served the Confederacy.
She married her late sister Eliza's husband,
James Clements.

Eliza Allen Clements, the daughter of Thomas Oliver Allen and Mary Garnette Tinsley Allen, was born May 28, 1827, in Tennessee. She died at home on November 26, 1899, and was buried at Mt. Horeb Church in Amherst County, Virginia.

James Clements, son of John Clements and Miss Anderson, was born August 4, 1823, in Amherst County, Virginia, and died at home on March 13, 1924. He is also buried at Mt. Horeb Church in Amherst County.
After the death of his wife Eliza, he married her widowed sister, Mary Jane Allen Whitten.

Devereaux Frederick Allen was photographed for *The News* (Lynchburg, Va.) during a 1903 reunion of the Amherst County Confederate Veterans. This copy of the old newspaper clipping was made by Bruce Jordan of the *New Era-Progess of Amherst County.*

The powder horn belonged to Richard Harrison Allen. The Colt revolver (on the left) carries the initials H.A.; it may have belonged to Richard Harrison or James Henry Allen. It fits the holster. The revolver on the right is an Adams. These artifacts, donated to the Amherst County Historical Museum by Stella Allen, were photographed by Bruce Jordan.

1861

TINSLEY LINSLEY ALLEN, BORN APRIL 1831, IS LISTED ON THE 1860 CENSUS as a farmer in the Buffalo Springs Post Office district in Amherst County, Virginia. The first of the six Allen brothers to go to war, he enlisted at Millner's Store in the western part of the county on August 15, 1861, when the Amherst Johnson Guards, also known as the Long Mountain Boys, were organized. This unit entered Confederate service for one year on September 24, 1861, and was assigned to the 58th Virginia Infantry when it was organized in Staunton on October 13, 1861.

Staunton offered some new experiences for the volunteers, who were primarily from rural areas, including a visit to the Western State Mental Hospital, which still operates on a hilltop outside the city.

Corporal Allen wrote the first letter of the collection from Camp Lee in Staunton. It reflects the enthusiastic expectation of adventure felt by many of the volunteers. In it he mentions Jack Coffey, a friend from Amherst who, with his own brothers, would join Harrison, James Henry and Thomas Allen when all would be conscripted into the 13th Virginia the following spring. He also mentions his cousin, Ellen Burford, and her husband Daniel.

October 14, 1861

My dear Ma,

I embrace this my earliest opportunity of answering your very kind letter which was the first time I have heard or received a line since I have been here. It gives me great pleasure to hear you all are well except Sister Eliza. She is very ill and I was very sorry to hear that she is so ill. This leaves me well. Hoping when these lines reach you they will find you all well.

I anticipated a very happy yesterday on going to church. I heard three sermons preached during the day and night and I also saw a young lady that I love very much. I have gone to church every Sunday since I have been here. Our fare is as good as might be expected. We have enough to eat—coffee, sugar, flour, bacon and beef.

Well, I shall change the subject, replying to what you ask of me. You stated in your letter of the 12th if it would be worth your coming out where I am. I can say this much, if I was sure how long we would be here I could say more about it. I expect we will stay here all the week or maybe longer. I do not know how long. I would be glad to see any one of you. Our camp is in sight of Staunton. There are good stables where you can let your horses stay, and any of the boys can stay in the camp, which will not cost anything, and if you come you can stay at the hotel where you will have a room to yourself and it will be much the cheapest to reside there.

[John J.] Jack Coffey stayed with us last night. I am glad to learn that Daniel and Miss Ellen have been up to see you all. Give my love to Ellen when it is convenient. Daniel came down to Charlottesville with Thomas Rucker Sunday. He said they were in great spirits.

I have nothing of importance to write and there never was anyone worse in writing a letter. I am this morning nothing but a [unclear] out and in. The boys look like they are wild.

Sallie, you say you have not heard from Mollie [Camden] since she left. She came to Staunton with us and the next morning started for home. I have received one letter from her since she left. She was very sick after she left for home. She is boarding in Richmond now. She said as soon as she got home she would write and let you all know how times were in old Richmond, etc. I will close this subject.

If you can't come, tell some of the boys to come about the latter part of this week. [If] they can start soon in the morning, they can ride to Staunton in a day. Coffey got here about 4 P.M. I would be glad to see any of you all at any time. Tell Thomas to come, it will not cost much, and he will see something that he has never seen. You have the privilege of visiting the lunatic asylum [Western State Hospital] where all the deranged people are. I was there for preaching yesterday. There is a winding pair of steps about four stories high which gives a delightful view of the town when on top. Well, I will close this subject. I have nothing more of importance to write. Give all the family my best love, etc.

Nothing more at present than remaining your devoted son,

Tinsley L. Allen

The volunteers from the relatively isolated rural communities of western Virginia had little natural immunity to the common diseases they met in the camp (measles, for example) and were stricken in great numbers. When the regiment was ordered to Highland County to join Stonewall Jackson's command, there were only about 400 effectives, and many men, weakened by illness and unable to march the full distance, had to be carried in wagons.

They went into winter quarters at Fork of Waters, Camp McCulloch. Tinsley wrote to his sister.

November 13, 1861

Dear Sister Ellen,

I embrace this opportunity to drop you a few lines to inform you of the times as they are and health, etc. We have a great deal of sickness here in the camp and death of one or two. I have been marked on the sick list this last week and sent to the sick house. I returned back to camp yesterday and feel tolerable well now, except the headache.

Mr. Jennings said you all were well. I should have been glad if some one of you had sent a few lines by him and let me hear how times are.

We are expecting orders every day to march to Romney in Hampshire County, a northwest course from where we are. 'Tis expected there will be a battle, but there is not much said about it. General Jackson has written to Col. [Edward] Goode of our regiment to issue no more furloughs for the present. We expect we will take winter quarters at Romney or Winchester. Romney [is] 80 miles and Winchester 100 from where we are.

They were fighting in Greenbrier a day or so ago and it is said our men gave them fits. Two of our picket guards were shot last week by a Union man and a very little boy. They rushed upon them and they ran upstairs and the pickets followed after them. They shot and killed one, wounded the other. The little boy shot one of the pickets. The pickets took them on to Staunton and placed them in prison.

Well, I have nothing of much importance to write more than remember my love to all my friends. Nothing more than remaining your brother,

Tinsley L. Allen

Col. Goode was a native of Bedford County and a graduate of the Virginia Military Institute.

From the same camp, he wrote to his mother a few days later.

November 22, 1861

My dear Mama,

I again embrace this earliest opportunity to drop you a few lines to give you a portrait of things in general. Times are very dull here in camp. The health is bad. We have 774 men in our regiment and out of that number there are only about 300 fit for duty. It makes it very hard for them that are able to stand. As for myself, I have recovered my health again. We have a great many sick in our company. We were in hopes we would leave, but we received orders to put up winter quarters and we commenced cutting and hauling lumber today, so it is likely we will stay here this winter.

We picked up two men today. They were trading northern money, giving 90 cents on a hundred. We all carried them before the colonel. He could not find anything wrong about them, so he let them go free. They could tell a great deal about the Yankees, how they were fixed, etc.

Well, I could say a great deal more, but having several more letters to write I shall have to bring this to a close.

If I was to tell you 50 of our men voted against Captain [William Aaron] Higginbotham, what would you think about it? It is so. He has gone to Amherst and we made up the roll and mailed it to Buffalo Springs, Amherst County, to the care of James Millner to read and to hand it to the captain. I do not know what may be the result.

I shall close by saying I remain your son until death,

                                                      Tinsley L. Allen

William Aaron Higginbotham was the captain when the company was formed at Millner's Store. He apparently survived this vote, as the records show him to be captain until May 1862, when he was not reelected. To brother James Henry, who hadn't entered the service yet, Tinsley added this note at the bottom of the same letter:

Dear Henry,

Permit me to give you a small paragraph this wet night for the first time, my dear sir. I would be more than glad to hear from you and all dear friends. You will please attend to my cattle best you can. Mr. Johnston will tend to the cattle until Christmas. You will see to them after that time. See that my fodder and stacks are not destroyed and also see that my horses are well treated. You shall not lose for your trouble. You know it is out of my power to see to them.

You will write to me as soon as you can conveniently do so and let me know how things are going on. Hoping these few lines may find you and dear friends enjoying the sweet blessings of this life, etc.

You will get my side of [unclear] from Tonley. As soon as

you can you will oblige yours.

Nothing more at present, so good-bye. Remaining yours respectfully,

Tinsley L. Allen

The regiment spent a quiet Christmas in camp. Although they had not yet seen battle, forty-eight men had already died, fallen to disease.

1862

ACCORDING TO THEIR SERVICE RECORDS, four of the brothers—James Henry (sometimes called Henry), Richard Harrison (called Harrison or Harry), Thomas O. and William P.—were all conscripted into service from the Amherst County militia and enlisted in Co. E of the 13th Virginia Infantry as privates on April 22, 1862, at Gordonsville in Orange County.

According to a letter from Harrison written six days prior to their official date of enlistment, William and James Henry were still at home. (Harrison signed all of his letters with his initials—R.H.)

April 16, 1862

My dear Ma,

I embrace this earliest opportunity this morning to answer your kind letter which came to hand on the 13th. It gave me great pleasure to hear from you all that you all were well. This leaves me well at present. I hope when these few lines reach your hand they may find you and all the family enjoying the great blessing of health.

I have nothing important to say at this time. I wish I could see you and all my sisters and brothers again like that. I would give anything in the world to see you all again.

We have an abundance of sickness in our camp at this time and some very uncertain deaths. I can't say how long we will stay here at this place. I don't think we will stay here much longer.

The law has passed that all over 35 years will be sent home.

I can't say what will be done with us. Some think we will be put into volunteer companies. I don't believe any man will know until we are mustered into service. We have a right hard time here standing guard and loading wagons and [railroad] cars. We have to guard anything if it ain't worth ten cents.

Well, Ma, we have prayer meeting every night and good prayers and a sermon. We have a place fixed perfect for the business, and every Sunday there is preaching at the church. I think there is a great call for it. Camp is a roughneck place as I ever was at.

Well, Ma, I must bring my few distressing lines to a close. I remain your devoted son until death,

R.H. Allen

Dear Brother,

I seat myself this morning to answer your kind letter which came to hand on the 13th instant. It gave me great pleasure to hear from you that you were mending. William, you request of me to ask V. Sandridge about that land. He said that Mr. Gooch was to get it. V. said that he was going to write to his wife about that and if Gooch don't take it you can get it. You go and see V's wife and she will tell you about it.

Arthur White sends his love to you. William, you must excuse me for not writing any more to you at this time as [unclear] is going to start.

William, if I was you and Henry I would [not] hurry myself to get in camp for you get worried of it. I want you and Henry to stay home as long as you all can.

Direct your letters to Gordonsville, Orange County, Virginia.

I close,

R.H.A.

Despite Harry's admonition to remain home as long as possible, William and Henry were in camp at Gordonsville when William wrote his first letter to his mother ten days later. He is unhappy about having been put into the 13th Virginia Volunteers, even suggesting that were he at home, he would sue to prevent it happening. He counsels his brother-in-law, James Clements, not to come to camp.

April 26, 1862

Dear Ma and Family,

I take pen in hand this morning to drop you all a few lines to let you all know how we all is. I has been sick ever since I has landed here. Me and Henry is with the rest of the boys. Our fare and weather has been the worst ever I has been acquainted with. Ja[mes?] is tolerable well at present. I know the worst thing when we came down here that I ever heard them say that they are going to put us into the Volunteer Company for during the war. If I was at home again, there is nothing would take me. Henry is [unclear].

We are now 7 to 10 miles from Gordonsville on [the] Rapidan River, where the Yankees is all around us. It would not surprise me if we was in a fight at any time.

If [I were] James Clements, I would not come down here. They is trying to treat us very unlawful. They [are] going to take us and throw us in the 13th Va. Volunteers for during the war and if I was at home I would try them, Ma.

I want you to try [to] see my corn [is] taken care of as times is going to be harder than ever we saw them. Ma, I would be glad if you could me a pair of shoes made. You can get sole leather from Mr. Whiteside. I will [send] my measure to be certain they [will be] long enough and be certain not [to] raise them too high.

If you all want to write to us, order them to Gordonsville, Orange Co., Va., Company E, Virginia Volunteers, to the care of Lieu. [Samuel R.] Luckett. I do not know how long we will stay here. I must close as the mail is about starting. I am in hopes this will find you all well.

Will close by saying your affectionate son,

William P. Allen

In an election held on May 1, Tinsley was elected second lieutenant of Co. F, 58th Virginia. On May 8, the regiment, part of the famous Stonewall Brigade, was involved in the battle of McDowell, in the mountains some sixty miles west of Staunton. In a letter written on headquarters letterhead from their camp near Winchester, he describes the battle and the pursuit.

May 26, 1862

My dear Mother,

'Tis with a grateful heart I embrace this earliest opportunity of answering your very kind letter of the 14th which gave me much pleasure to hear from you [that] family and all dear friends was well. This leaves me well at present though I have been very unwell some days back and was hardly able to march.

I have been on a march every [day] since the 9th of May. I haven't rested but two days during that time.

We commenced hitting the Yankees and on the 6th of May. Haven't rested but two days during the time we commenced fighting the Yankees the 7th of May in Augusta at Rogerers & on the 8th the great Battle of McDowell that was the greatest fight I ever experienced or ever I want to experience.

I was in the whole engagement, the first firing was at our company and two others. We came within eighty steps of the Yankees before we saw them. They fired upon us before we were aware of them. It is a wonder they had not killed us all. They wounded [James] Orrandorf and cut 3 bullet holes in his coat at the time. He was one of my company killed. Several other men in other companies [were killed]. During the fight our company had 2 or 3 wounded. But I cannot see how the men came out as well as they did for the [minié] balls were [as] thick as drops of hail. I never want to be in another such battle again if it can be helped.

We ran them down into Pendleton County at Franklin. They was firing upon us with a cannon, but we did not mind that we had taken a great deal from them. We found we could not get another chance at them so we returned and never stopped at all. [We] went on after the other ones and after some several days march we overtook them and commenced [firing] on them and been fighting them 4 or 5 days. Killed a great many and taken so many prisoners [that] I can't say how many we have taken.

Sunday morning we had another stout battle, that was yesterday morning. I never heard cannon roar so in my life. We were not engaged in that, but I was there at the time. The [minié] balls fell all around me. The boys did not get in it either. They got there at the time the Yankees were retreating. They had some [of] the fun of running after them. We ran them five miles out of Winchester. They burnt some large [store]houses of goods. As we were running through the town after them I never heard such rejoicing among the females in all my life. [They were] running to the streets with great quantities of all kinds of things to eat and waving their handkerchiefs. The road was full of clothing for both men and women.

[A piece of the paper has been cut away, possibly by a stamp collector, leaving gaps in a couple of sentences in the next paragraph.]

I heard our people [missing] them below Richmond [missing] I do not know how [missing] I do hope it may be [missing].

We have lost a great many men out here in this fight. But we have whipped them without a doubt and have taken a long train of wagons and horses they had taken, our Negroes made fires of them. I saw one yesterday myself [that] we had taken [while I was] walking by the side of a Negro woman that they had taken. They have taken a quantity of Negroes in this part of the country. Well, I shall close the subject.

The boys are well at this time. I hope I may see you all soon. I have not heard anything of J[ames] Whitten. Give my love to all of my friends. I remain your devoted son until death,

T. L. Allen

According to company records, Thomas was reported absent, sick, in May and June 1862. If he returned to his regiment in June, he may have wished he'd remained on sick leave.

In June the 13th and 58th Virginia were involved in battles at Cross Keys and Port Republic, suffering heavy losses in both Valley battles. In mid-June they rested briefly, then marched through Jarman's Gap in the Blue Ridge to Mechum's River, west of Charlottesville, where they boarded railroad cars for Frederick's Hall and Beaver Dam Station, northwest of Richmond. Their target was Gen. George B. McClellan's Union army north of the Chickahominy River. They met them on the 27th, at Gaines's Mills.

The 58th was sent in to attack one of the strongest Union positions. The fight was brutal in the Chickahominy swamps, but the 58th, in concert with the other Confederate regiments, prevailed. Their pursuit of the fleeing Union army ended on July 4, near Charles City Court House outside Richmond.

Tinsley wrote to his sister Sallie and their mother during a badly needed day of rest for the 58th. Both letters share the same piece of paper, but their tenor and content are wildly different.

July 6, 1862

Dear sister Sallie,

I embrace this opportunity to answer your very kind letter of the 26th which was handed to me yesterday by Mr. Coffey, in which I was very glad to hear from you and all dear friends. I am very glad that you have the luck to hear from your D so often, and glad to hear cousin E[llen] was up to see you. I was very glad to hear from her. I gave a letter to Henry Coffey for her and he dropped it in the office at Amherst Court House. I received a letter from you and her the other day, dated April 3rd. You must give her my love. I heard D was wounded.

Dear Sallie, do you ever hear from Mollie Camden of late? I was in her old neighborhood the other day, but all of the folks have left their homes. I have not heard from her for many days.

You asked me if I got a letter some week or two ago. I did

not. I started on to you, this before I left the valley.

Harrison is here now. He is complaining of being sick. I am much displeased with this section of the country. It does not agree with my health. The water is so bad.

Well, I shall have to close. May this reach you enjoying the blessings of this life and I may see you soon.

So good-bye,

T.L. Allen

In his letter to his mother, he describes the recent battles and mentions having seen Harrison.

My dear Mother,

'Tis with a grateful heart I embrace this, my earliest opportunity of answering your very kind letter of 26th of June which came safe to my hand yesterday by Mr. Coffey, [in] which I was more than pleased to hear that all the family and all are well.

My dear Ma, I have travelled until I have naturally worn out. Since the 6th of May I have marched the rise of 500 miles. We have nothing but a little meat and crackers. I am so worn out on them [that] I can't eat, for I have nothing that I can eat. I have become so weak that I can hardly get along. I have fallen off to nothing. May the Lord of Mercy smile upon us and bring this great war to a close, for if ever there was a poor one worn out in camp I am one. It appears that I would give anything to go home, but there appears there is no chance for me to get home.

We don't do anything of late but fight the mean Yankees. We have been after them since Thursday a week ago, now 11 days. We have run them 27 miles below Richmond. I was in the Friday's fight. It was one of the greatest fights ever I saw. The 2 lines of battle [stretched] some 4 or 5 miles and the ground was covered with dead men from one end to the other, with our men and Yankees, but the Yankees were much the greatest, I think. We had one killed dead in our company and a great many wounded. Bob Mc[unclear] was badly wounded. We are within the hearing of the Yankees now close [by] at their camps.

I saw Harrison a few days ago. He was well. He was in the same fight as I was, but not beat. A man's life don't look like [much of] anything here.

Well, dear Ma, I must change the subject for my pen is so indifferent I am afraid you will never read it. I should be more than glad to see you all, but I do not know when that will be, and if we should not have the privilege to meet on earth again, may we be prepared to meet in Heaven. I trust you will make preparations for that great day, for I see no pleasure here.

Give my love to Mary and all of the children and all of the family at home. So nothing more at present, more than remaining your devoted son until dead.

So farewell!

                                    Tinsley L. Allen

P.S. I cannot tell you where to direct your letters unless you direct them to Richmond, for we are marching every day.

Six days later, Harrison wrote to his mother from Henrico County, near Richmond. He spelled it "Henryracker," which may have been as much commentary as mispelling; the Chickahominy was spelled "Chickenharmer." He, too, described the battles of Gaines's Mills and Malvern Hill.

                                    July 12, 1862

My dear Mother,

My dear, this being my earliest opportunity of answering your kind letter that was on handed to me the 6th instant. It affords me great pleasure to hear that you all are well. This leaves me well excepting [that] I am nearly broken down and my legs are wearing out. I hope when these few lines reach you they may find you enjoying great blessings of health.

Ma, we have had a hard time down here in marching and

fighting. Ma, we had a great time on the 27 of June. It was the greatest slaughter with men that I ever saw in my life. We had 4400 hundred in our regiment [the official records put regimental strength at 250 at Gaines's Mills] and we lost [unclear]25 killed and wounded. It was a great time. We went in about 4 o'clock in the evening. We had to lie on the battle field all night. It was a sight for anybody to look over the field the next morning.

The first day of July was another great day. We went in the fight not until night and we then marched down into the Yankees before we knew it. Col. [James A.] Walker stepped up and touched one on his shoulder and asked him what regiment did he belong to. He told him, and Col. Walker told him to fire away and he made his escape by telling them that. We only got 2 men killed and 3 wounded that we know of. Lt. [Samuel] Luckett got knocked down by a piece of [unclear].

We have had some hard times since we've been down here. I was starved for the want of water. It is a spare place for water down here. I waded in the mud up over my knees where we forded. The mud was very bad in the Chickahominy swamps.

Well, Ma, I will change my conversation. Ma, you don't know how bad I want to see you all. I would give anything to see you all and if I didn't study so much about home I wouldn't care, but [it] looks like I can't help from thinking about home. All the Amherst boys have left but me and James Coffey as well.

Ma, you stated in your letter that you wanted me to have my likeness taken and send it to you. I am sorry to tell you that it is not in my power to have it taken. We are in camp about 3 miles from Richmond. I can't say how long we will stay here. If I can get a pass tomorrow to go in town I will have it taken and send it to you. I wish I could have it taken, for if you want to see me as bad as I want to see you, it would be a great satisfaction to you, dear Ma.

I am sorry that our letters are so long [in transit] before they land. I received a letter from you the 6 of July, one that you sent by Mr. Coffey, and one came by the mail. You state in that [one] about having so much rain. We had a great full wet day after the fight.

Well, Ma, you said your wheat looks well. I am glad of that for the people are destroying everything down here. It looks a sin to see how everything is going to destruction.

Well, Ma, I must come to a close. Please excuse my bad spelling and writing as I am on post and I am pressured very much. Give my love to all dears, sisters and brothers. Tell them may God grant that I may be spared to come home to see them again. Nothing more at present, still I remain your devoted son until death,

R.H. Allen

The next day, still in "Henryracker County," Harrison wrote to Devereaux, the youngest Allen brother, who was still at home.

July 13, 1862

Dear Brother:

I seat myself this Sabbath morning to inform you a few lines to let you hear from me. This leaves me well at present and hoping when these few lines come to hand they may find you in the same blessing of health.

Little brother, I wish I could see you, but we are far apart, but I am in hopes it won't be long before we are together again.

We had [the] greatest day Friday and Tuesday that you ever [could] think of. The fight that we had in the valley was a great fight, but it was nothing compared to this. We were thrown into the line of battle, stood under the firing of the cannon for 3 hours. I thought I would be struck every minute. The [unclear] got killed there and one wounded by a [unclear].

Dev, I received a letter from my old T[ulark?] the 8 of this instant. You ought to have heard it read. Dev, give my love to Sallie and Ellen and tell Sallie that I saw the division [of] Daniel's unit, the regiment that he belongs to, but I did not see him. I must close. Good by,

R.H. Allen

James Allen was home in Amherst during July, although we don't know if he was on furlough or sick leave. He wrote a brief letter to his brother Harrison, on one side of a sheet of writing paper, but did not send it off immediately.

July 18, 1862

Dear Brother,

I take pen in hand to write you a few lines to let you know I am not so well. I have been very poorly with a sore throat and headache but thanks be to God I am [a] great deal better.

Dear Harry, I am hoping when these few lines come to hand they may find you enjoying yourself very much. Harry, they say the militia time is out the 16th of the month. I am in hopes you all can get home. I know you all have had a hard time down there in the time of the fighting and marching, for I know [a] little something about it myself.

Well, Harry, I will tell you something about our crop. We are through harvesting and I tell you our wheat is splendid. We will make 150 or 200 bushels of wheat, and our corn looks very well. [As to the] wheat, there is one [thing], they all did not plant much. Our potatoes look very nice indeed.

Harry, you must write [as] soon you can and tell us all about your great battles. Give my best respects to James Coffey and tell him all his folks are well. Dear Harry, I will soon have to close my remarks. Hoping this may reach you safe and find you well. Thomas sends his love to you and said he wrote to you while he was out in the western parts.

I still remain your affectionate brother,

James H. Allen

Four days later, Ellen took advantage of the other side of the same sheet of writing paper to add her message to Harrison. She mentions the death of Greenville C. Camden, the captain of Tinsley's Co. F, 58th Virginia, who was killed at Gaines's Mill.

July 22, 1862

My dear brother Harrison,

I once more take my pen in hand this Tuesday evening to drop you a few lines. This leaves us all well and, my dear brother, I hope when these few lines come to hand they may find you well and doing well.

Oh, Harry, I have felt so much for you in the time of that great fight below Richmond. I feel thankful to the good Lord that you and poor Tinsley both came out safe. You ought to try and put your trust in the Lord and he can help you and protect you.

We have had some very [unclear] deaths. Poor Dabney Whitten died last Friday evening and was buried Saturday. I was to his burying and his funeral. Old Dr. Staton died last Saturday and was buried Sunday. I was so sorry to hear of Capt. Camden being killed. It seems there are a great many deaths, those at home and in the camp.

Well, Harry, we received your letter last night dated 13 of this month and it gave us much pleasure to hear from you and to hear that you were well and sorry to hear of you being most broken down. Ma and Henry wrote letters the 18th of the month and thought they would be sent by Sam Staton, but he says he is not well yet, and so we will have to send them by mail.

Daniel Burford is here and says he will carry them to the Court House and have them mailed. Daniel says he will write to you next week. Daniel's eye is out. I suppose you heard of him being wounded in the eye. He is quite [unclear].

So, Harry, I will have to close as my paper is out. I still remain your sister,

E. H. Allen

P.S. Ja[mes] Whitten and Mary send their love to you.

James is very sick. He has been sick ever since he came home. He said he would write if he was able.

E.H.A.

At this point there is a break of more than two months in the letters. During that period, on July 17, Tinsley was elected first lieutenant of his company. The 13th and 58th were engaged in the battles of Cedar Mountain (August 9) and Second Manassas (August 28-29). On September 5, the brigade crossed the Potomac into Maryland, then crossed back on the 11th. On the 14th they captured Harper's Ferry, taking large stores of northern goods, then again crossed the river and headed toward Shepherdstown, where they participated with heavy losses in the battle of Antietam on September 17.

Both regiments were near Martinsburg, in Berkeley County, when Tinsley describes the capture of Harper's Ferry and the battle of Antietam to his mother. He mentions John Allen, a corporal in Co. F, who had enlisted at the same time and place as Tinsley and was probably a relative. The optimism expressed in the letter was, unfortunately misplaced. Wounded and captured on September 17, John Allen died of his wounds ten days later.

September 22, 1862

My dear Ma,

I embrace this, earliest opportunity of dropping you a few lines to inform you of my health. This leaves me well after a very long march. After leaving home I marched into Maryland before I caught up with my company and have been on the march ever since. We marched back into Virginia and to Maryland again, so I have crossed the Potomac four different times. We had a very hard battle in Maryland [Antietam]. Thank the Lord I came out safe once more.

John Allen was wounded in the hip and left in Maryland. We left in such haste we could not bring him. You tell his mother the doctor said he did not think it is dangerous. He thought he would recover.

We had a battle at Harper's Ferry [the battle of South Mountain] this day, that is a week ago, and took 10 or 12 thousand prisoners and 46 pieces of cannon. General [Samuel] Garland was killed there. We were there. I have been marching and fighting ever since I left home. Two nights is the longest I have stayed at once place since I left.

I should have written to you and friends before this time, but we have had no chance to mail letters. I don't know when I can mail this.

I saw Harrison as I was going to my company in Gordonsville. He came from Richmond that morning and they left him there. He was sick. I suppose it was well he stayed there, for I have had a time of it since.

It was ten days before I overtook my company after leaving home. I saw Thomas and Henry this morning. Henry has been sick for several days but he is going about again. I have not heard from one of the family since I left home. I am hardly able to say where [it] would be best to direct your letters, for we are always on the march. I suppose Winchester, Berkeley Co., Va., Com. F, 58th.

Here is a few lines for Mr. Gooch enclosed in my letter. You will give it to him.

(The lines just mentioned are missing from the letter and were, presumably, sent on to Mr. Gooch as requested.)

I have nothing of great importance to write this morning. I am in much hurry, expecting orders to march every minute. I should be more than glad to see you and all dear friends. I have not heard from William since he left me at Amherst Court House on Sunday evening. You will write as soon as this comes to hand and let me hear from you all dear friends.

I have many dangers to encounter here, but may the Lord be with me while here on earth and guide and shield me from the harrows of this vain and unthankful affair which I am placed in now. If it should be my fate never to meet my dear friends on earth, may we meet in Heaven where pain, trouble and sorrow will never be felt and [there will be] fear no more. May the Lord be with you all is my prayer for Christ's sake.

So I shall have to close my few unimportant lines. Give my love to James and sister Mary and all her family, to James and sister Eliza and family and tell them to write to me soon. Sallie, you and Ellen must write soon. Give Miss Ellen B. my best love. May these few lines reach you all enjoying the sweet blessings of this life and I may hear from you all soon. So nothing more at present, more than remaining your devoted friend until death,

Tinsley L. Allen

There is another gap of two months in the family correspondence. During that time the 13th and 58th spent a fairly quiet time in camp in Clarke County, Virginia, near Berryville and Millwood, and later near Winchester, in Frederick County. Their main activity was the destruction of rail lines around Martinsburg and Front Royal.

New recruits and the return of convalescents bolstered their ranks. A letter from William, who had apparently been home on furlough or sick leave and had just returned to his regiment, reveals an entrepreneurial bent. It was written from camp near Cedarsville in Clarke County, where four of the brothers were again with the 13th Virginia.

November 19, 1862

Dear Ma and Sisters,

I seat myself this night to drop you all a few lines to inform you of my health. I am quite well at present. Hoping when these lines come to your hand they may find you all well and enjoying yourselves as well as usual. Dear Ma, we landed at Staunton Tuesday night after leaving home and we landed at Winchester the 9th and we stayed there all night and reported, and they returned us back to Front Royal, and we found them near Cedarsville, about 12 miles from Winchester. We traveled at least 2 hundred miles before we landed to our regiment. We traveled 2 days in snow and it was as disagreeable weather as I ever traveled in. I landed to my company the 11 November and my company was very glad to see me.

I am well satisfied with my officers. I am very well satisfied with my captain. He allows us as many privileges as I could ask him. He has allowed us to forage every day. I can leave camp and make 5 to 10 dollars. Ma, if we could meet with anything to sell, we could do well.

I traveled about 12 [miles] today and I came across 1 bushel of apples. I paid 5 dollars for them and sold them for 14 dollars. Ma, me and the boys labor 10 times as hard as we ever labored at home, and I am in hopes that I will get paid for my trouble.

Henry and Tom and Harry are doing well at present. As we get only half rations, we will have to try and make out.

Tell Devy to get every one of the apples that he can as apples are selling so awful high. Ma, if we stay here long, I want you to try and send a load of apples to us.

Well, Ma, I will bring my few lines to a close, as it is very dark to write tonight. Sallie, you must excuse my bad writing. Tell [unclear] Little and Liza and Joe I [still] have some of their chestnuts they gave me. Ma, give sister Mary howdy for me, also sister Eliza. Ma, as it is so dark I must close. I will write you again soon and I will let you all hear all of the news.

Ma, you all must write to me soon. Direct your letters to Winchester, 13th Reg., Co. E, of Ewell's division. Sallie, write all of the news. I must close as I am in a hurry. I will close by saying I still remain your true affectionate son to death.

So farewell,

William P. Allen

At the end of November the 13th and 58th were ordered eastward, toward Fredericksburg, but there was such a shortage of clothing that the barefoot men were held back, Thomas and James Henry among them. Harrison left the regiment on December 4, near Fredericksburg, and was sent to Chimborazo Hospital in Richmond, to recover from a reaction to a smallpox vaccination. He wrote to Sallie from the hospital.

December 9, 1862

Dear Sallie,

It is with great pleasure that I do seat myself this morning to inform you of my health. This leaves me well excepting my arm, where I was vaccinated. It got coal in it and it is the worst arm that I ever had. It [is] all inflamed. I can't raise it to my head to save my soul. I sincerely hope when these few lines reach you they may find you enjoying the great blessing of health.

Dear Sallie, I wish I could see you all at this time. I ain't heard from you all since I left home. I would like to hear from you all very much at any time.

I left the regiment the 4th day of this month 14 miles from Fredericksburg. William and Tinsley were well when I left. Thomas and Henry was left at Orange Court House as they was barefooted. All the barefooted was left there. I ain't heard from Thomas, since I heard that they had gone home, but I can't say.

Well, Sallie, I have nothing important to write at this time. These times are very hard down here at this place. There is a great chance of getting sick in Richmond. The smallpox is all over Richmond. I could get transferred to Lynchburg if it weren't for the smallpox. They won't grant no furloughs on account [of they are] fearful that you would carry the disease in country.

I am at the hospital at Chimborazo, the third division ward. If my fare is a little bad, I can put up with it though.

Well, Sallie, I must come to a close. Give my love to all the family and inquiring friends and receive a large portion for yourself.

R.H. Allen

P.S. Direct your letters to Chimborazo Hospital, 3 Division Ward at Richmond, Va. And if I am gone they will be sent to me at my regiment. But send the news and letters.

On the back of the same sheet of paper, he wrote a second letter, to Ellen.

Dear sister Ellen,

I will take this present opportunity this evening to drop you a few lines [to] let you hear from me. This leaves me well excepting my arm. It is so sore, indeed it is the worst arm that I [have ever] had in my life. It is a running sore from my shoulder to my elbow. I can't raise it to my head.

Dear Ellen, hoping when these few lines reach you they will find you enjoying the great blessing of this life. I wish I could see you all, but I reckon it will be some time before I will see old Amherst again. If I live until spring, I want to come home if I can. I don't expect to get off any sooner.

Ellen, I have no news to write at this time. Times is hard about here. You can't live very well if you spend about 5 dollars a day. I ain't drawn no money yet. I can draw any day that I want, but I don't expect to draw any till I get ready to go to my regiment. I [owe] money [to] so many different persons [that I am] afraid. I expect I will draw 75 or 100 dollars. I am due over 100 dollars. I drew part of my money when I was with the regiment, but I ain't drawed that amount yet.

Well, Ellen, I must come to a close. Tell Mama and Devereaux they must excuse me for not writing to them. Give my love to them and to Mary and family to Eliza and other Clements and tell them to write to me and let me hear the news.

R.H. Allen

Direct your letter to Chimborazo Hospital, 3 division ward c/o Richmond, Va.

The great battle of Fredericksburg took place on December 13. Both the 13th and 58th Virginia regiments were involved, but William was the only brother to participate, as the barefooted Thomas and Henry were left behind and Harrison was hospitalized. The day after the battle, Harrison wrote to William, using the formal salutation in common use at the time, even among family members.

December 14, 1862

Dear Sir,

It is with great pleasure that I do seat myself this Sabbath morn to drop you a few lines to inform you of my health. This leaves me well excepting my arm, and it is sorer than when I was with the regiment. My elbow is the sorest place I ever had. It is in a running sore from my shoulder to my elbow. I have suffered mightily from pains all over these past nights that I don't sleep hardly any at all.

I wish I could hear from you. I heard that you all were fighting at Fredericksburg, but I did not hear any particular news about it that you might rely on. The papers state that the enemy [is] across the Rappahannock.

William, I have nothing important to write at this time. Times are very hard here. There is a great chance of sickness in Richmond at this time. The fare is very hard here. There are so many sick in this place [that] they can't be tended to as they ought to be.

I don't know when I will come [back] to my company. As soon as I can I am coming.

William, I want you to write me word when we were put in the company. I expect I will draw some money before I leave. I think I was put in the first day of April. I want to be sure of it, and I want you to write me word how you all are getting along. Let me know where Thomas and Henry are in their camps as soon as you get this if it is in your power.

Well, William, I reckon I might as well come to a close. I wrote home on the 9th of this month. If you get a letter from home for me I wish you would send it on to me. Give my respects to Tinsley and all the boys and Thomas and Henry if they are there, but I don't think they are with the company. I would like to hear from you all very much indeed. Since the battle I am in hopes none of you all ain't hurt no way.

The smallpox is very bad in the place. They won't transfer anybody nor grant furloughs, no discharges on [account of] the smallpox getting spread about.

Well, write as soon as you can. I will bring my few lines to a close. Give my respects to all inquiring friends and receive a large portion for yourself.

R.H. Allen

P.S. Write soon. I can get my money before I leave. I want to be certain what time to draw from.

The 13th went into winter camp along the Rappahannock, about five miles west of Port Royal, where the pickets exchanged pleasantries, food and news with the federal pickets across the river. The 58th went into camp near Guiney Station.

1863

The 13th Virginia spent the first three months of 1863 in camp along the Rappahannock without the services of any of the Allen brothers. According to the official records, James Henry and Thomas had been absent without leave since November 29, 1862. William was absent sick from December 23 until the following March 1. Harrison had been transferred from the hospital in Richmond to one in Farmville, Virginia, in December. The first letter of 1863 is one that Harrison wrote to his mother.

January 15, 1863

My dear Mother,

It is with much pleasure that I do seat myself this morning to answer your very kind letter which came to hand yesterday. It was dated the 5th inst. It afforded me great pleasure to hear from you all and to hear that you were well. This leaves me in reasonable health. I have been very unwell but I am better at this time. Hoping when these few lines reach you they may find you and all the rest of the family enjoying the good blessing of this [unclear] life.

Dear Ma, I would be glad to see you all at this time. I reckon it will be some time before I will get in old Amherst again. Well, Ma, I have no news worth your attention to write. Times is very hard at this place. There is a good deal of sick[ness] here but there are not as many as there was when I first came. There have been several cases of smallpox here.

Mama, you said you hadn't heard from me for some time. I

wrote you a letter since I landed here. I got here the 21st of December. I received your letter which was dated the 16th of Dec. I received it the 20th. This last letter was remailed at Richmond and sent to me here.

Well, Ma, you said that William has landed at home. He had better luck than I did. You said he had a very bad arm. I think me and him was vaccinated out a poison scab. I was in a bad fix.

Well, Ma, you said something about sending me a box of vittles, but I don't want you to do it as it is uncertain whether I would get them or not. Our fare is very bad here, but never the less, I can make out. Well, Ma, as I want to say a few words to Sally and Ellen, I will come to a close. Give my respects to all the family and receive a large portion for yourself.

R.H. Allen

On the same piece of paper, he wrote to his sisters, making some cryptic references to the Yankees.

Dear sisters Sally and Ellen,

I will take the present opportunity this morning to drop you a few lines to let you hear from me. I am in reasonable health at this time. I truly hope when these few lines reach you they may find you enjoying the great blessings of this life.

Dear sisters, I wish I could be home with you all. I could enjoy myself so well with you all. I hope the day is to come when we all can be at home free once more.

Sallie, I ain't heard what has become of D since I left home. Ellen, I expect the Yankees is got S[unclear], for they say they is fighting there and they took a heap of our men prisoners. There was a carload of Yankees just here yesterday where I was taking out [unclear].

Sallie, you said something in your letter if I want it would kill me fighting. I won't say any more.

Well, Ellen, tell Dev to save me some apples 'til I come home if he pleases.

I must come to a close. Give my love to all the family, receive large portions for yourselves. I still remain your devoted brother until death.

R.H. Allen

P.S. Write soon and direct your letters to Farmville, Virginia, 3rd Division, Ward B, to the care of B.H. [unclear name]. I received a letter from Thomas B.H. Woodson yesterday.

The 58th Virginia also spent the winter camped along the Rappahannock. Tinsley was in camp in Caroline County, Virginia, when he penned this to his brother William, who was then at home.

January 21, 1863

My Dear Brother,

'Tis with a great deal of pleasure I avail myself of this opportunity [of] answering your kind letter of the 10th inst., [in] which I was very glad to hear from you that you landed at home safe and that your arm was something better.

Dear William, I did not write to Harrison as you requested of me. In a few days after you left I heard that he had been transfered to Farmville. I did not know his ward, so I thought it useless for me to write.

We are in the same camp you left us in. I enjoyed a very dull Christmas and I suppose Christmas was over when you landed at home. I have no news of importance to communicate.

We have to go on picket down on the Rappahannock River. We have to go about every ten days. It is about 9 miles from our camp. It is on tidewater. The Yankees is on one side and we [are] on the other or its bank. Two of our men got on a skiff the other day and [there came] a puff of wind and drove the vessel to the other side of the river and the Yankees got them.

Today is very wet. We have to go on picket tomorrow. I fear we will have a bad time of it. We have to stay 2 days and nights.

I saw your captain last week. There was no letters for you. Your friend Lockwood was very sick.

You will tell Ma if she hasn't done it to send that money to Colemon for the hire of Negro Daniel [at] the first opportunity. I should be more than glad for that to be settled.

Well, I must bring my few lines to a close. I expect to send some money by Mr. Toler. Nothing more at present. Remaining yours,

Tinsley Allen

Tinsley also wrote to his sister Ellen from Caroline County. Most of the date has been torn away from the page, but the number twenty-one can be made out. The penmanship and paper are nearly identical to the above letter to William, so we might assume it was written on the same day in January.

Date unclear

Dear Ellen,

I embrace this, my earliest opportunity of dropping you a few lines to inform you of my health. This leaves me well, hoping these few lines may reach you enjoying the sweet blessings of this life. I was very glad to hear from you that you was well and doing well. I weighed this morning and my weight was 217 lbs.

Well, dear sister, I have nothing of importance to communicate. Times is dull. I should be very glad to see you and all the family. You must write soon. I must bring my remarks to a close.

Remaining your brother until death,

T.L. Allen

A couple of weeks later, Tinsley wrote again to William, this time suggesting that if he were to bring some spirits with him when he returned to the unit, he would not go unrewarded.

February 6, 1863

My Dear Brother,

I embrace this my earliest opportunity of answering your very kind letter of the 2nd inst. which gave me great pleasure to hear from you and all dear friends that you were much better. This leaves me well. Hoping when these few lines reach you [they] may find you all dear friends enjoying the sweet blessings of this life.

I have nothing of importance to communicate. Times is quite dull in camp. I am very sorry that it is out of my power to be with you all about the 10th. But I am in hopes you all will enjoy yourselves well. I have never mentioned it to the Col. nor anyone else. I thought it was not worth my while doing for I did not expect I could get off.

Dear William, you said you had a barrel of whiskey making. You said you would try and bring me a dram down when you came to camp. It would be very agreeable with me if you would bring down some 2 or 3 gallons. We would buy it off you. You could box it up so as it would not be trouble. Try and bring along a little, anyhow. Bring me a little separate if you can.

Well, I must change [the] subject. If you should not come to camp soon, you must write and let me hear how you all [are] and write soon and give me all of the news and let me know if the conscripts is called out or what has they done.

Give my regards to all of the family and share a portion for yourself. Your sincere brother until death,

T.L. Allen

None of the letters indicate what family event Tinsley missed on the 10th of February, but Harrison apparently obtained a furlough from the hospital, as he complains in his next letter of having a hard time getting back to Farmville and warns his brothers (who were AWOL at the time) to avoid Lynchburg as travel papers were being closely checked.

February 19, 1863

My dear Mother,

It is with great pleasure that I do seat myself this morning to inform you of my health. This leaves me very well at this present time. Hoping when these few lines reach you they may find you and all the rest of the family enjoying the same good blessing, etc.

I [started] my journey last Monday night [at] half past 8 o'clock. I had to stay in Lynchburg one day. I seed a good many of my old acquaintances. I saw Nat Higginbotham, Luther Brown, Bob Brown, John Coffey.

Ma, I haven't no news to write at this time. I like to get bothered in my return. I had to go to the provost marshal's office and get a passport before I could get on the cars.

Ma, tell the boys if I was in their place I would not come by Lynchburg when I went to camp for if they can't get good papers to show they will be taken up for sure. There were 3 men arrested on the cars last Sunday night, and [they] was put in the guard house in Lynchburg. It is hard for a man to get through Lynchburg.

Well, Ma, give my love to all the family, to sister Eliza and family and Mary and family and Ellen. Give my best love to Miss T.B.P.

Ellen, if you come to Lynchburg, try and let me know when you will come.

As I ain't got any news to write at this time, I will bring my few lines to a close. Nothing more at present. Still remain your devoted son until death,

R.H. Allen

P.S. Write soon and let me hear the news. Write me word when you expect the boys will leave.

William's sick leave ended on March 1, but his return to his regiment included a stay in the Lynchburg jail, reasons unknown. A letter written from Lynchburg puts blame for his predicament on two compatriots, and he mentions John B. Deverbe of Co. D, 2nd Virginia Infantry, who was on detached duty in the quartermaster department at Lynchburg. Dick Tankersley, who operated a tavern in East Lexington, is also mentioned.

March 4, 1863

Dear Ma,

I seat myself this morning to drop you a few unpleasureful lines. I feel unwell this morning, most expecially since I heard this morning I have to go to Richmond. We will have to start this evening at half past 4.

Old Deverbe told me twice that he was going to send me from here to my regiment. Now the old fool has taken up the notion to send me to Richmond with the rest. Ma, I will tell the truth, I would not have go to Richmond for 5 hundred dollars because I think I has seen my portion of punishment here. I would rather be dead this morning as to be in the condition I am in.

I am in hope that Bev Mason and Jes Richson may not live to return to their regiment [unclear]. They has been the occasion of me being punished for nothing.

We has been half starved ever since we has been here. I am in hopes we will not have many days to stay in Richmond. We may not have more than 2 or 3 days to stay and again we may have to stay 1 or 2 weeks.

I expect to try very hard to come home after I get to my regiment. I would be more than glad to get home if I could not stay more than 3 days and I expect to make an effort to come if I have to live in the woods after I get there. Before I would be taken again I would run the chance of being shot.

Ma, if Henry has not gone to his regiment yet you tell him I want him to bring me some whiskey down when he comes down. I want him to bring me some 3 or 5 gallons without fail. Tell him to go over at Tankley's [sic] and get it out of my corn whiskey. I has a five gallon keg over there. If he brings it, tell him to make a box to exactly fit the keg and to fill the keg full so it will not rattle, and if he cannot bring it I would be glad if you would send it by some other good chance. Tell those who bring it to just take it on the same coach that they ride. I would like to get something down there to sell to get some of my money back for what this trip will cost me.

Ma, if you think it would be the best to keep the whiskey you can do so if you keep it. As soon as it is all done you had better send over and get it and put it away for safe keeping. Tankley [sic] promised me a barrel to put it in. I would have been glad if I could have tended to my business myself, though I am going to try to return in a short time again.

Ma, I will have to close as my paper is nearly out. I am in hope these few lines may find you well. You all need not be uneasy about me for I will try and do the best for myself I can.

I will close by saying I still remain your most true and affectionate son until death,

Wm. T. Allen

On March 16, James Henry wrote to his mother and sisters, one letter on each side of the paper, from Guiney Station, where the 13th was still in winter camp with the rest of Jubal Early's division.

March 16, 1863

Dear Ma,

I embrace myself this morning of dropping you a few lines to inform you of my health. These few lines leave me well at the present. I am in hopes when these few lines come to hand they may find you enjoying the same health.

Ma, Capt. [Andrew Jackson] Eheart is not the man I took him to be. He reported me to the colonel and all the boys. He is [unclear] for that thirty dollars but my captain says he will try and see into that himself. So I am in hope we will not be docked in our wages.

Ma, if Eheart comes to your house I want you to treat him cooly, trifling [unclear].

Well, Ma, I am going to leave this company if I can get off. I want to join the cavalry.

Ma, A[rthur] White is in the guard house yet. I think he is getting tired of it.

Ma, Tom sends his love to you all. He is well.

Well, Ma, I must bring my few lines to a close. I will remain your devoted son until death.

James H. Allen

Dear sister Ellen,

I seat myself this cold foggy morning to inform you [of] my health. I am quite well at the present. I am in hopes when these few lines come to hand they may find you enjoying the sweetest of life and also all the family.

Ellen, times is hard down here. [If] we get anything here, we have to pay for it. House rations is very scanty. I have to buy flour every now and then or suffer a gnawing that can't be.

Ellen, we [are] looking for a fight at Fredericksburg. Now every day the people is leaving town, getting out [of] the way. But I am in hopes the Lord be for me, that is a day I hate to see come.

Well, Ellen, how you and Tom is getting along? Is you seen him since I left home? I expect you have. Ellen, you have a fine little [word blurred]. You must tell him to write to me and tell me all the news.

Well, Ellen, I must bring my few lines to a close by saying I will remain your affectionate brother until death. Write soon.

James H. Allen

Harrison was not doing very well in the Farmville Hospital. His ailments seem to have expanded beyond the problem he had with the smallpox vaccination.

March 24, 1863

My dear Mother,

I will embrace this being my earliest opportunity this morning to inform you that I haven't been well for some time.

I have been very poorly for several days with the headache, also my leg has pained me very bad since I wrote you last. I am a good deal better at this time and, dear Ma, I am in hopes when these few lines is handed to you they may find you and all the rest [of the] family enjoying the great blessings of this worrisome life.

I would be glad if I could see you all at this time. You don't know how bad I want to see you all. I am tired of this place. I don't know whether I will get to come home before I go to my regiment or not. The board hasn't sat since I came from home.

I would be glad to hear from you all. I ain't received but one letter from you since I left home. This makes the third letter that I has wrote to you all. I would be glad to hear from William. I would have gone up there if I hadn't looked for the board round.

Well, Ma, I haven't no news worth your attention to write to you. Times is dull and hard. We has had a very cold snowy time. It was a very bad time on the sick. We didn't have neither wood or coal for two days. It is nice weather now. When I hear the knee deep howling every night it reminds me so much about home. I feel like I ought to be at home.

Well, Ma, I will bring my few remarks to a close as my headache [is] very bad today.

There is a good many stirring around today as it is a fast day.

Ma, give my best to Ellen and Devy and tell them I want to see them. Tell Ellen she is to write to me. I would be glad to hear from you all at any time. Give my respects to sister Eliza and her family and sister Mary. Also to [blurred] and Caty.

Nothing more at present. Still remain your devoted son 'til death,

R.H. Allen

P.S. Please write me as soon as you get this. Direct your letters in the care of Mr. Ladd.

A week later, Harrison started a letter to his mother, but despite his reassurance as to his well-being, he was depressed. He finished it two days later.

April 10, 1863

My dear Mother,

I seat myself this morning to drop you a few lines to let you hear from me. This leaves me very well at this time.

. . .

My dear mother, as I started to write you the other day I got despondent, [so] I will embrace this present opportunity this Sabbath morning of answering your very kind letter which came safe to hand a few minutes ago. It affords me a great deal of pleasure to hear from you all and to hear that you was well. This leaves me very well at this time excepting my leg is very weak, yet it is getting better. It is a good deal better than it has been and I sincerely hope when these few lines reach you they may find you all the rest of the family enjoying the great blessings that this life can afford you.

Dear Ma, I would be gladdest of anything in this world if I could see you all at this time. Oh! how glad I will be when this war will come to a close so all the poor soldiers can return to their respective homes where they can be treated like humans.

Ma, you said something about me getting a [furlough]. As the thing is turn out, as it is I don't look for one. I['m] sure I would get one as easy as anything if Doctor Gardiner hadn't to list his examination of me and took my name down for a discharge. The doctor that [is] tending the ward I stay in don't care what becomes of a man. The board sat last Friday and there was 2 furloughs, 2 discharges, 14 sent to their regiments. The doctor said [the board] will set again before long. I will go before them. I reckon if I could [have] went while doctor Gardner had been here I would have been at home, for he told me that I won't [be] fighting for certain.

Well, Ma, there are [a] good deal sick up here and deaths, but thanks be to the Lord my health is very good if it weren't for my leg. I am in hopes it won't be long before I can stand to walk on it as well as I has.

Ma, you said something about coming down here to see me. I would be the gladdest if I could see you. But it is an uncertain place to come to for anybody. I may get to come home yet. If I don't get off any other way I will try to get 4 days.

I am sorry my paper is given out as I ain't half wrote as much as I want. I wrote a letter to Henry last Sunday and I wrote to him to write me word if they expect to march soon. If they didn't, I had an idea to go to my regiment.

Ma, excuse my short letter. I will try to do better. My love to all the family,

                                                                   R.H. Allen

James wrote to his mother from the 13th Virginia's camp near Hamilton Crossing in Spotsylvania County, near Fredericksburg.

                                                                   April 13, 1863

Dear Ma,

I seat myself this morning to answer your kind and affectionate letter which came to hand [the]12th inst., which affords me great pleasure to hear that you all was well.

Dear Ma, thanks be [to] the Lord these few lines leave me well as common, only excepting a very sore mouth that is a camp disease. Most every man in our regiment is complaining about [a] sore mouth and sore throat.

Ma, I haven't got much news to communicate with you this time, only time is as hard in camp as ever. We is still looking for a fight yet down here.

Ma, you stated in your letter that Ann Marston was dead. That was a very sudden death. I was very sorry to hear of it, and you said Brock Patson was dead, too.

Ma, I received a letter from Harry [the] seventh of this month. He said in his letter he had been complaining with his leg. He said in his letter that he was very tired of that place. He said he could not march. I wrote to him to stay on as long as he could because there is some danger of being in a fight here. I wrote to him I [was] wishing I was in his shoes, anywhere else except in the army.

Ma, I heard there was a good many cavalry in Amherst. I reckon they will eat and steal every[thing] they will get their hands on. I am in hopes they won't interfere with anything of yours.

Ma, give my respects to Mary and her family and sister E[liza] and her family. So, no more at present, only I remain your devoted son until death.

James H. Allen

William, in camp with James, wrote to his mother on the same day.

April 13, 1863

Dear Ma,

I seat myself this morning to answer your very kind letter which duly came to hand last evening of [the] 7th inst., which it found me very well at present. I was glad to hear that you all was well and do sincerely hope when these few lines come to hand they may again meet you in good health.

I saw Tinsley this morning and handed him the note you sent to him, and he was well as common. He was glad to hear from you all. I began to think that you all had forsaken us entirely.

Ma, we have no news of importance, everything is just about like when we wrote before. The army seems to be on a stand at present. There has been some fighting not far from us a few days ago. We will be apt to have a fight in a short time here. There are too many men here not to fight, and we are in talking distance from the Yankees.

The old men has not gotten off from here yet. They all got out of the guard house at one time, though they has put them all back [in] again. They has brought a suit and now I do not know when they will get off. There are about a dozen of them in the guard house.

I saw Tinsley is here. He says as soon as he gets off, he is coming up to see you all. He has bought where old Mrs. Flood used to live. I reckon he will be a neighbor to you all [in] another year.

Ma, you was saying something about my whiskey. I am glad it is still [there], although I think he ought to have made more out of the grain than you said he did. Ma, if you are wanting any money, you had better sell some of it. Whiskey is awfully high here. It sells for $16 to $20 a quart here, though I have not tasted a drop since I have been here. We can find ways enough to spend our money without spending it that way.

We have been trying to get Henry's regiment, though I think it is doubtful about getting it. Ma, I am going to try and get to come home as soon as I can. I would be more than glad to see home again, although when I come home I expect to go and join the cavalry. I see we has got to stay in service, and I am going to try and have my choice where I will stay. They don't want men to go into the cavalry. I expect when I go I will have to run the blockade.

I wrote a letter to Col. [E.H.] Swinney asking a few days ago belonging to the regiment I want to go in. I expect to get an answer in a few days.

A good many of us are going down to the crossings tomorrow to have our pictures taken. If you all see my little Lark with mine, don't be surprised at it. I am just going to have it taken with my army suit on.

Ma, give all the family my love and also Eliza and Mary and [unclear]. I will close for the present by saying I still remain your affectionate son until death. Write soon.

Amen,

William P. Allen

About two weeks later, Thomas wrote to his mother and reported that Tinsley had been hospitalized with a sore leg. The official records show him as having gone on sick leave on April 17.

April 26, 1863

Dear Mother,

I seat myself to let you hear from me. This leaves me well at this time and doing as well as could be expected and I hope when you get this it may find you and all of the family enjoying the same good blessing.

Dear Mother, you must excuse my long delay of writing. I received your kind letter some time ago but I did not answer it for the boys was writing to you and I thought it [would] be best for me to put it off until now. So I expect to answer all letters I get while I am in camp, but I have no news to tell you at this present time.

Times is hard here and I reckon times is awful hard in old Amherst. I got a box from my wife last week. I was glad to get it.

Brother Tinsley was sent to the hospital yesterday. His disease was a sore leg. He was well [as] to [his general] health. All of the boys is well and send their love to you all.

Ma, you must tell Mr. Clements he must not think hard of me for not writing to him. You all can see the same letter, and tell sister the same. You must give my best respects and love to all of them. Tell J. Clements I hope he will not have to come to the war, for I don't think he has no right to come as [unclear] is here.

A[rthur] White is joined the 58th Va. Reg. All of the old men will be at home.

This week we are yet in camp and I can't say where we will go, but we expect a fight here some time soon. I expect to come home some time this summer if life lasts to see my wife and you all. Tell Devy howdy for me and to make all he can this year. I am sorry for him.

I will send you some money as soon as I draw.

Well, I must close by saying I remain yours truly,

T.O. Allen

Arthur White's record shows him to have enlisted in Co. E of the 13th in

April 1862,deserted in May of 1862 and been discharged on May 1, 1863 on a writ of *habeus corpus*, but no details are given. White was thirty-eight years old at this time. Many soldiers swapped places with men in other regiments, and White may have done so.

Gen. Hooker's Union army began to stir in late April and the Confederates met them in the great battle of Chancellorsville, where Stonewall Jackson was fatally wounded, and again at Fredericksburg at the beginning of May. The 13th and 58th Virginia regiments fought together in Gen. William "Extra Billy" Smith's brigade. William describes the battle to his mother in a letter written a week after the battle. He mentions a Yankee observation balloon.

May 10, 1863

Dear Ma,

I will seat myself this morning to drop you a few lines to inform you all of my health, etc. I feel very unwell this morning. I have taken a very bad cold, I suppose it is by exposure.

Thomas and Henry are well at present. I do sincerely hope when these few lines reach you all they may find you all in the best state of health.

Dear Ma, we has [been] seeing an awful hard time for some ten days and also has been under the fire of the cannon and the musket for that length of time. We has been in 2 awful dangerous fights besides all our dangerous skirmishing. We has been in several small skirmish fights. It was said that we was in a dangerous fight last Sunday as ever was fought. It was in a large field and we charged right up on them and we had it breast to breast, though after a time the enemy fell back. Captain [Samuel or Daniel] Fields was killed dead in his spot. He was shot in the head with grapeshot which [made] all of his brains run out. I was awful sorry that [he] got killed.

There was several more wounded in our company out of our regiment. There was about one hundred killed, wounded and taken prisoner. We has lost several men since we has been fighting, though old General Lee says he has won the largest victory ever has been since the war has been going on.

We has taken an awful sight of prisoners a few days ago. The number was ten thousand, though General Lee says the whole amount will be very great.

The report is [that] General Jackson got his arm shot off and he is very low from his wound. It was one of our own men who shot him through a mistake. He was across the picket line and they thought he was a Yankee.

Tinsley is not here. He was sent away on account of having a very sore leg. I cannot tell if they sent him home or not. Him and Harry may thank their God that they was not here in the time of all this fighting.

It does seem that we can't go through what we have again unless some of us would get killed. I am in hopes that we may never have such a time to experience again.

The Yankees [have] gotten very close to Richmond and burnt a great deal, such as bridges and mills, which they came very nigh of cutting off our supplies. It was several days that we could not get any mail.

The Yankees captured two thousand of Negroes over here and [have] taken them back with them. Such trips as that I think pays very well. It would not surprise me if they will aim to cross over in a short time again as the old balloon was up yesterday and is up again today.

In the time of the fight there was a lot of the 58th taken as prisoners, which I believe they wanted to be taken. [Reuben A.] Rube Stinnett was taken. At one time I come very nigh being taken myself. The Yankees' loss is twenty thousand; our loss is estimated at ten thousand. So is our latest accounts.

In the time of the fight I lost everything I had. My knapsack was robbed and everything taken out.

Ma, give Eliza and James and also give Mary my respects, also their children, and tell them I am in hopes that I will get to come home in a short time. I would give any sum in reason to get to come home to see you all, though I cannot set any time when I can get to come home.

Ma, you all must write soon. It seems like you all write very seldom. It has been a long time since we have gotten a letter from you all. I received a letter from Sallie some ten days ago. When you all write, give me all of the news.

Arthur White is well and sends respects to you all. Charley Henderson got wounded and their company is throwing into another company. Charles McDaniel also got wounded. The boys is looking for Hugh Burks [to come] back.

Ma, give all the family my kind respects and tell Devy to try and do the best he can in the way of making a crop. I will have to close as I feel very unwell.

I still remain your true and affectionate son until death [to] a man,

William P. Allen

Harry wrote to his mother from Farmville on May 18.

May 18, 1863

Dear Mother,

I deeply sympathize this present opportunity of answering your kind letter which came safe to hand yesterday, and it affords me great pleasure to hear from you all. This leaves me very well at this time excepting my side. I suffered very much last night. [The] doctor said my liver's [intergation?] on that side has been very badly swollen. But I feel right smart this morning.

Dear ma, I hope when you get this it may find you and all the rest of the family enjoying the good life.

Dear Ma, I would be so glad to see you all. I [unclear] if I could get home to stay. I think I could live so happy. But I hope I will live to see this unhappy war come to a close yet. Ma, I would be so glad to hear from the boys. There has been some very hard fighting [where they are]. I see in the papers that old general Jackson got his left arm shot so bad he lost it. As he got shot the [ball] passed through his right hand.

There was a great loss on both sides as well.

Ma, you was saying something about Daniel coming down
to see me, but it would cost him right smart and maybe I can
get to come home after a while. They are sending men off to
their regiments as fast as they get well and before [unclear]
here a few days ago. It was [unclear] that the Yankees was in
[unclear to end of letter].

The 13th Virginia spent the rest of May in camp at Hamilton Crossing.
During that time a movement grew to have the regiment transferred to
Jeb Stuart's cavalry brigade. The men were enthusiastic, and the ordnance
sergeant went so far as to inventory their weapons to ascertain how many
were suitable for cavalry use.

William mentions the hoped-for transfer in a letter to his mother
written from Hamilton's Crossing. He also tells her that Thomas and
James Henry have been court-martialled for having gone AWOL over the
winter and are awaiting punishment, and he uses the term "running the
blockade," a euphemism for being absent without leave.

May 21, 1863

Dear Ma,

I again seat myself to drop you a few lines to inform you all
of my health. I am only tolerable well at present. I has been
very unwell for some 2 weeks. I am very ornery about being
sick. I am afraid it is some kind of fever working on me.

In the time of our fighting we had to expose ourselves
enough to kill anybody. We remained in a line of battle for 8
days with hardly any sleep at all and the cannon balls and shells
[were] flying over us and in[to] our men every second besides
musketry. It was said that our regiment made some as brave
charges as ever has been made. Capt. [Daniel or Samuel] Field
got killed in one of our charges. Old Gen. Jackson also is dead.
We miss him awfully. There was [an] awful slaughter of men
here in the time of the fight. Our loss was said to be 10
thousand. We certainly lost that many and I believe our loss
was more than that. The Yankees' loss is said to be 30

thousand.

I would be glad if I could say that all of our fighting was over, although it is my opinion that we will have a heap of hard fighting to do this summer. It would not surprise me if we have a fight here again in a short time. The Yankees has reinforced 50 thousand here so much hard fighting is enough to dishearten any person on either [side].

If I could get to come home sometimes I would not care so much, though there is no chance to get to come home at this time unless a man would run the blockade and that I do not expect to do. If I was to run the blockade, I certainly never would come back here.

Night before last there was 6 of the Amherst boys left. Last night there was 6 more left, and there is some ten or fifteen talking of leaving again tonight, all of the 49th. Pink Davis and his set has gone. They started a detail after them last night. The detail will land before they will.

Our colonel is trying to get our regiment into the cavalry. He has petitioned the department. We are looking to hear every day. We will be apt to hear this week. Gen. Stuart is very anxious for us to get to come to his cavalry. If we get to go into the cavalry it will be apt to give us a chance to come home.

Henry is very anxious to come home. Tom and Henry has had their trial, though I do not know what it will amount to, though I judge they will not do anything with them more than take some little of their money from them.

We are getting enough meat at this time, though I do not know how long it will hold out. So God knows I would rather be at home and live on my dry bread as to be here and get the best [I] could be furnished with. I expect to come home some time this summer if I do not die or get killed, though our lives is so uncertain here.

Devy, I will send you some gun powder by Robert McDaniel. You can use it as you want it, though don't waste it. I would send some other things, though I reckon it will be out of his power to bring them. I drawed my money today and I would be glad to get a chance to send some of it home.

Ma, Henry Stinnett brought our socks to us and one apple apiece and also some tobacco. I would be glad if you had a chance to send us some tobacco. It is so scarce here and high, from 3 to 4 dollars a pound and I cannot do without it and it is not fitten to chew.

I am in hopes that you all may get this letter soon as it seems you all have such bad luck in getting our letters. I saw a note from sister Ellen. She said that you all had not heard from us since the fight. Me and Henry is always writing letters to you all, though we cannot hardly ever get a letter from you all unless some person pass[es it on].

Ellen, if you want to see my picture, if you go and see N. T., she will show it to you. She sent me word it had landed safe. I hear from her very often. About the time of our fight I received a very affectionate letter from her. I had to sympathize very much.

Well, Ma, I will have to close. I do sincerely hope when this letter comes to hand it may find you all well and doing well as [my] heart could wish. I still remain your affectionate son until death. My obediences to you all.

William T. Allen

On April 30, Col. James B. Terrill blocked the unit's transfer to Stuart's cavalry, creating great disappointment among the men. William wrote to his sister from camp at Hamilton Crossing.

June 1, 1863

Dear sister Ellen,

I will seat myself this morning to write you a few lines to inform you of my health. I am as well as common at this time and I do sincerely hope when these few lines reach you all they may find you all enjoying the greatest of health and happiness that can [be] bestowed upon you all.

Ellen, we received you all's letters a few days ago which they was about 3 days agetting here. Our mail here ever since the fight has been awful unregular, which I do not believe that you all gets half the letters that we write to you all. I saw one published in Richmond written in your name which I expect it is one that we started to you. I will try and send these and get it out if I can. Thomas and Henry is both well at this time.

Henry wrote a letter to Ma yesterday and started this morning which I reckon he posted her with all of the news. We received marching orders yesterday. We are looking to leave here any minute. We are looking for another fight every day. There are thousands of Yankees just across the river. I am afraid that we will have another dreadful time here again. I dread the day when we will have to march in another fight. It seems like fighting does no good. What I would give if this war was over. There is no enjoyment for men here.

Our papers has returned from Richmond for our regiment to go into the cavalry. Now old Col. Terrill is so contrary he won't sign the papers. Our officer has been cutting up awfully about it. There is 3 companies [that] say they will leave the regiment if he does not sign the papers. He may take a notion to sign them. Our captains came around this morning to know who could furnish horses. If we could get to go in, it would give us a chance to get to come home to get horses. I do hope we can get in. It will be decided very soon. It is our only chance to get to come home.

It is not worth a man's while to talk of leaving here now. They would sentence [him] to [the] penitentiary for 5 years or shoot him if he was to leave without good papers. There is a man to be shot here today at 4 o'clock for deserting and going home. He is from Amherst. His name is James Wilmore, belonging to the 49th Va. Regiment. He is willing to die. He was ra[unclear] yesterday. There is some more that has ran away from that regiment. [They] will be shot if they catch them. I heard they had caught Joe Colemon and [put] him in Amherst jail.

I am going to try and get to come home some time this summer if I cannot come now.

Ellen, I sent a letter to Ma by Rob McDaniel and I also sent Devy some gun powder by him. He said he would bring them up to you all. If he has not brought them up [words missing].

Tom and Henry has been court martialled. They took their pay from them while they was not here and one more month extra which was 4 months pay taken from them and 9 extra duties. I call this a poor unjust war.

Ellen, we received a letter from Sallie a few days ago. She was well. I also received one from Miss Ellen [Burford]. I was very much surprised to get a letter from her. Ellen, you wrote to me to know if I had lost my little Tulark's picture or not. I have not lost it yet. As it happens when I lost my things I had it in my pocket where I carry it every day.

Ellen, you spoke of being over to see cousin [Mer?]. I was very sorry that you failed to see cousin [Newley?] as she seems like she is so anxious to see you. She was over near Lynchburg the last time I heard from her. Ellen, I suppose you saw my picture when you were down. I expect you heard a great deal when you was down there as cousin E. likes to talk so well.

Ellen, give Ma and all of the family my love. Give James Clements and sister Mary and their family my respects. I will close for the present by saying I still remain your kind and affectionate brother until death.

William P. Allen

Harrison got a furlough from the hospital in June, and while he was at home in Amherst County, he wrote to his brothers, who were still with the 13th Virginia.

June 6, 1863

Dear Brothers,

As this brings me to my earliest opportunity this even[ing] to drop you a few lines to let you hear from me. This leaves me only tolerable well. I have been very unwell for some time. I have had a spell of fever since I have been at Farmville. I ain't altogether well of it yet.

I got home last Saturday even[ing] on 10 days leave of absence. My time is out Sunday, which is tomorrow. Dr. Smith, he reported for me today as I want [to wait] a while [before] I go back. I suffered right smart last night with the pain in my side. I can't say when I will go back. As soon as I get better I will go back to Farmville. I don't expect to stay there long when I go back.

Dear brothers, I would be glad to see you all, dear brothers. I earnestly hope when these few lines reach you three they may find you all well.

Henry, your letter came to hand last night. It affords me great pleasure to hear from you all since the battles. I haven't no news to write to you all at this time. Sallie and Daniel is here now. They join me in sending their respects to you all, so all of the family sends the best respects to you all.

Well, as my paper and pen is bad, I must bring my few lines to a close. Please excuse my bad writing and spelling, as I am very incapacitated. Nothing more at present. Still remaining your devoted brother until death,

R.H. Allen

P.S. Please write soon as I would be glad to hear from [unclear words].

The 13th left camp on June 5 and headed back to the Shenandoah Valley, where they recaptured Winchester from Gen. Robert Milroy's Union army. The 13th was detached from the brigade and assigned to provost duty in Winchester, where they were able to get clothing and other supplies. They remained there until they rejoined the army as it retreated from the great battle at Gettysburg on July 5–6. Part of the 13th was detailed to take Union prisoners to Staunton; James Henry was part of that detail. He wrote to his mother from New Market.

July 9, 1863

Dear Mother,

It is with great pleasure that I seat myself this even[ing] to drop you a few lines to let you hear from me. I am yet only tolerable. I have a very sore arm. I was vaccinated and it is all inflamed and turned into a running sore. When I get back to Winchester I am going to report to the doctor and I am going to try for a furlough. I am going to try to get home any way.

When I was down to Staunton with the prisoners I wanted to come home so bad. I was so close by home and to start back to old Winchester so far from home.

Well, Ma I am in hopes when these few lines come to hand they may find you & all enjoying good health.

Dear Ma, our soldiers has had another dreadful battle in the State of Pennsylvania. The road is full of the wounded passing to Staunton. They say there was a large loss on both sides. Ma, I was very glad I was just right where I was. That was one fight we escaped.

Ma, I will close. Give my best respects to sister Eliza & her family & to sister Mary & her family and to sister Ellen H & to Devy & receive a large portion for yourself.

Ma, write soon. I haven't heard from you all for some time but I expect when I get down to Winchester I will meet with a letter from you all. I am in hopes, anyhow. Ma, direct your letters to Co. E, 13th Virginia Regiment, Ewell's Division. Write soon.

James H. Allen

Tinsley was in Richmond, still on sick leave, when he wrote to his mother on July 11, although his regiment was near Williamsport, Pennsylvania, protecting a supply train. He was not hospitalized but boarding with a civilian, and the opening lines indicate that he had just returned to Richmond from a leave of absence, possibly at home.

He, too, spoke of the battle of Gettysburg and was concerned because he thought his brothers had faced that awful danger.

July 11, 1863

My dear Ma,

I embrace this my earliest opportunity of dropping you a few lines to inform you of my health. I landed here on Sunday evening safe. [My] arm is well. As to my legs, they is something better. Hoping these few lines may reach you and all of the family enjoying the sweet blessings of this life.

I have been boarding at Mr. Good's since I left home. Very nice people.

I have nothing of importance to communicate. There has been a great excitement here in the city, fear of the Yankees, but [it] is calm at this time.

There has been a great fight in Maryland and Pennsylvania. Our losses has been very great indeed from all accounts. I can't hear the particulars of the battles. I should be more than glad to hear from the boys. Poor fellows, we may judge they have had a hard time of it. I trust the good Lord may be with them in all of their trials while here on earth. I haven't heard from them since they left Winchester.

Well, I will change my subject. When you write, let me know whether Harrison has returned to the hospital or not. I haven't heard anything from him since I left home. And let me know how you are getting on with your crop. Did you get your harvest saved? We have had a great deal of rain for the last week or so. You will please excuse me not writing sooner. I will try and do better hereafter. You will write soon.

We had 2 deaths here in the city yesterday by accident. One shot himself and the other was drowned in the James River. They are fixing today to send after the wounded. The Yankees has been all around the north eastern side of Richmond.

Well, I have nothing more of importance to write, so I will close. Give my love to all my of my sisters and brothers and tell them they must write soon and have a portion for yourself. Direct your letters [to] Richmond, Virginia.

Remaining your devoted son until death,

T.L. Allen

Tinsley's next letter was written a couple of weeks later, to Ellen. He had not yet heard from the boys and was still concerned that they might have come to harm at Gettysburg.

August 2, 1863

My dear sister Ellen,

With a grateful heart I now embrace this, my earliest opportunity of dropping you a few lines to inform you of my health. I am something better than when I left home. Hoping these few lines may reach you and all dear friends enjoying the sweet blessings of this life.

Dear Ellen, I have nothing of importance to communicate. Times [are] quite dull and very hard. There is no reason in the price of things about Richmond. Everything is out of date. I bought a horse the other day. I thought I might make a small speculation on him. While I am spending so much I should like to make some if I could.

Dear Ellen, I should be more than glad to hear from you and dear friends. I have not heard from any one of you since I left Amherst. I can't see why it is that I don't get a letter from some one of my friends.

Dear Ellen, you will write as soon as the respects of this come to hand so I may hear from you once more. You will give me all of the news. Let me know how Devy is getting on with his crop and how times is in old Amherst.

Dear Ellen, I haven't heard from the boys since the battle at Gettysburg, Pa. If you has heard from them, you will let me know. I am more than anxious to hear from them. I don't know whether they is dead or alive for I have not heard a word of them. I have spent some very uneasy hours about them.

I have deep sympathy for the soldiers. I know they have a very hard time of it. 'Tis to be hoped that we will have peace soon. 'Tis thought that France will interfere and recognize our independence. If she will do that we will have peace very soon.

Well, I have nothing of importance to write so I will bring my subject to a close. Give sister Eliza & James and family my highest regards, also sister Mary and her family, and also Ma. If I thought I would not be fit for duty soon I would try and get to go home, which I could do very easy, I reckon.

Well, I have give the general news, so I will close for the present. May this reach you and dear friends enjoying the sweet blessings of this life.

Still remaining your devoted brother until death,

T.L. Allen

Finally, Tinsley received a letter from his mother that told him that William and James Henry were safe.

August 6, 1863

My dear Ma,

I embrace this my earliest oportunity of answering your kind letter of the 2nd instant which came to hand the 5th [and] which gives me great pleasure to hear from you and the family that all was well. This leaves me as usual. I was very glad to hear being this was the first letter I have received from any one of you all since I left home. I am very glad to hear that William got H[enry] home for a few days.

I have no great news to communicate more than times [are] very hard. I was at Mr. Baler Martain's [sic] the other day. He sends his best love to you and the family. Mrs. Martain is paralyzed. She can't talk to do any good, has been for 3 years. I have also been at William Martain's. He looks as usual.

I should be very glad to get to see you and all. If I do not get fit for duty soon I shall try and go to see you all again soon. If I thought I should not been fit for duty by this time I should of tried and of gotten to of gone home before this time.

I am very glad to hear that you got your wheat crop saved for flour is very high and everything else is in proportion.

I have not heard from the boys since I left home. I should be very glad to hear from them. You stated in your letter that my trunk was at Amherst C.H. If it should be convenient for you to get it home you can do so, and if not it makes no [difference]. I may want it in the army again. I can't say. So it['s] where it's safe, that's all right.

So I will close. Give my love to all sisters and brothers. Nothing more at present. Remaining your son until death, so good bye,

T.L. Allen

Harrison had finally returned to duty on July 1, and he and William were in camp near Orange Court House when they wrote to their mother on August 31. Harrison's letter takes up about three-quarters of the sheet in his large handwriting. William's note is squeezed into the little space left at the bottom.

August 31, 1863

My dear Mother,

I take pen in hand to inform you a few lines to let you hear from me. This leaves me and all the boys well at this time and hoping when these few lines reach you they may find you and all the rest of the family enjoying the great blessing of this life.

Ma, I haven't no more worth your attention to communicate with you at this time. We are in camp between 7 and 8 miles below Orange C.H. We have a great deal of drilling to do here every day. I can't say how long we will stay here. I haven't heard no orders about leaving yet.

Our fare is only tolerable good. We can make out and that is about all.

Ma, you requested on me when I went to Farmville to let you know if I got all my clothing. They all was there and safe excepting my tobacco, and [my] ink was made use of as well as I can remember. All my other things was there.

Dr. Talliafaro said he didn't receive the address [that] I sent to him, but he said he remembered about get[ting] one report if no more. He asked me how I had been and I told him and it was all right.

Ma, tell Ellen all my old mess was all gone but Anderson. He was there. He was very glad to see me. He said he thought

I was dead. He was very sorrowed to see me leave. If he can't get a detail he has to go to his regiment.

Ma, I would be glad to see you all at this time, but I am afraid it will be some time before I will see you all again. It is hard for a man to get from here. It is reported that they're going to muster all the army in service for 5 years. I can't say whether it is so or not, but it is one thing certain, I don't expect to stay in 5 years. That is one thing certain, if I live I hope the war may be over before that time.

Ma, William received a letter from you the other day which was dated the 23 inst. I was glad to hear from you all and to hear that you all was well. Ma, I want you to write me word how times is in old Amherst, whether they got up many men yet or not. I heard the guards had shot Pink Davis. I would be glad to know if Henry had got home or not.

Well, Ma, as I haven't no news worth your attention, I will bring my few lines to a close. So give my love to sister Mary and family and also to sister Eliza and Mr. Clements. Tell Mary she must write to me. Ma, write me how Mary's crop is. Give my love to Ellen and Devy and tell them I would be glad to see them.

Nothing more at present, still I remain your devoted son until death,

R.H. Allen

Dear Ma,

I will write you a few lines to inform you of my health. I am tolerable well at this time and I do hope when these few lines reach you they may find you and all of the family enjoying the best of health.

Ma, I have no news of interest at all to write at this time, thought I would write you a few lines as long as Harry was writing. I wrote you a letter a few days back and I also received one from you and Ellen a few days back and was glad to hear from you all.

Ma, you wanted to know what I would be willing to take for

Luce. As times is there, I cannot tell what she ought to bring. Money is worth so little she ought to bring a large sum of it. Ma, I expect Tinsley will be home in a few days on a furlough and he can use his pleasure in selling her. It is my opinion it would be the best plan to carry her to a public place and put her up to the highest bidder. Good horses is bringing from 5 to 8 hundred dollars. I cannot tell what I would be willing to take for her unless I was there to see how horses is selling. If Tinsley don't come home soon, I will write again soon and let you know something more about it.

I will have to close. Yours,

William T. Allen.

One of the letters written by Harrison to Ellen is dated September 19, but the year has been torn away. It was written in Orange County, and very likely was written in 1863. Pieces of the page have been torn away and several lines have missing words.

He indicates concern that a major confrontation is brewing, but in fact the month of September passed rather quietly, with only sporadic skirmishes between the two armies on opposite sides of the Rapidan.

September 19, —

My dear Sister,

I will embrace this present opportunity this even[ing] of dropping you a few lines to inform you of [my] health. This leaves me well at present. Hoping these few lines may reach you and all the rest of the family enjoying the great blessings of health.

Dear Ellen, I would be glad to see you all at this time. I hope the time will come again so I can see you all. I would be glad to hear from you all at any time. It has been some time since I has heard from you all.

William has received letters from Ma since I [missing]. That is all the time that I has heard from [missing]. [Missing] to Ma in a few days after I landed [missing].

Ellen, I haven't no news to communicate at this time, no

more than [missing] for a fight here. But thanks be to God they
haven't [missing] persons yet. But I think we will have a fight
here before long.

Well, Ellen I will change my conversation [missing] will give
you the particulars of it. Ellen, I heard that [missing] and
Henry has gotten home. I was glad to hear that they had
[missing]. I know they was like me, they wanted to see home.

Well, Ellen, as William is waiting on me and it is getting
late, I will have to close as I suppose he will give you all the
news.

Give my respects to all the family, also to sister Eliza and
Mr. Clements and sister Mary and family.

Nothing more to say at present. Still remaining your
devoted brother until death,

R. H. Allen

Harrison's next letter, to his mother, is dated October 30 from Brandy
Station. Like the previous letter, the year is missing and so are some pieces
of the page, but we know that the 13th, after spending several weeks
maneuvering around the area, finally went into winter camp on property
owned by John Minor Botts, about three miles north of Brandy Station,
on the rail line.

October 30, —

My dear Ma,

I will this even[ing] inform you a few lines to let you hear
from me and all the boys. This leaves me and the rest of the
boys well. My dear Ma, I do sincerely hope these few lines may
find you & all the rest of the family well. Ma, I haven't any
news worth your attention to write at this time. Times is very
hard. That is no more than you [missing].

Ma, I reckon you [missing] the letter that me and Henry
[sent] to you a little while back. Alford Gooch [sic] is going
to start home in the morning. I thought I would write a few
lines and send [them] by him. But it is getting so late I can't
write as much as I would wish. So I will also send one hundred

dollars by him so you can see him and get it and make use of
it if you stand in any need, for you is welcome to it. If you don't
want it you can save it it for me and Mary. I may have a use
for it some day or other. But if you want it I want you to make
use of it. Well, Ma, as it is getting so dark [I] will have to bring
my few lines to a close. Give my best love to all [missing] and
to sister Mary and Eliza & Mr. Clements. Nothing more. Still
remain your son,

R.H.A.

The final letter of 1863 was written to Sallie Allen by Elijah M. Hogbert,
a native of Amherst who was in the 2nd Rockbridge Artillery, from their
camp in Orange County.

November 18, 1863

Dear Miss S,

I seat myself this morning to write you a few lines for the
first time. This leaves me well and hoping that these few lines
may reach your person enjoying a portion of the same health.
I am in hopes you will not think hard of me addressing with a
fresh as we have had but a slight aquaintance. I would like very
much to see you & all of my old Amherst acquaintances, and
as I cannot enjoy that pleasantry I would like very much to
hear from you & to hear how you are getting along.

I would like very much to get a furlough about [unclear] to
go home and if I do not but it surprise you if I [unclear] you
to visit [unclear] by furlough. I hope you will answer my letter
and give me the news and let me know who is married and
what has become of Miss Bette Sandridge and Miss L. Brinks
and Miss [unclear] White and give Mr. Arthur White and
family my respects. I would like to hear when Arthur is
[unclear]. He is a great favorite of mine and also Mr. James
Clements. I am told he is doing business for D[?] Smith. Tell
him to write to me and give him and his family my best respects
and also to Mrs. Whitten. I was very sorry to hear of Mr.
Whitten's death. I seen him in Harrisonburg the 5th of May

1862 and he was complaining of not being well then.

Preston Lawhorne was killed on the 14th of last month. He was a member of this same company that I am. He was a man that the company respected very much and [unclear] and a good soldier. We lost our cannon in that day and 3 killed and 13 wounded out of our company. We are to be sent back to recruit up. I suppose we will not get guns this winter. I believe that I have written all the news I can think of at this time. Direct your letters to Richmond, Va., 2nd Rockbridge Battery, Maj. McIntosh & C. Bertelman (?), 3 [unclear].

Yours very respectfully,

Elijah M. Hogbert

P.S. Please excuse mistakes and bad writing.

1864

The first letter of 1864 was written by Harrison, from the 13th Virginia's winter camp at Somerville Ford on the Rapidan. He and Henry were in camp; William was at home on leave.

February 25, 1864

My dear Mother,

It is with great pleasure I do seat myself this morning in regard of answering your most kind letter that came safely to hand this morning. Dear Ma, it affords me great pleasure to hear that you all was well. Dear Ma, this leaves me well as for common. Dear Ma, I do hope these few lines may reach you and all the family enjoying the great blessing this can afford you all. I haven't no news worth writing to you at this time. Times is about as [unclear]. Dear Ma, I would be glad to see you at this time. I reckon William is at home by this time. I reckon me and Henry will get a furlough when William['s] time is out. I would be glad to hear from him to hear what he done down to Richmond as he said he was going by Richmond to attend to some little business. I would be glad to hear how he come out.

Well, Ma, you said they had [unclear] Pink Davis. Poor fellow, he will be shot I expect. Capt. Hasley [sic] said he was going to have him shot. I['d] rather never see [it] come to this. His company is to see him shot. I don't care how mean any person is, I don't want to see him shot in this war for I know how it makes the home folks feel.

Well, Ma, you said Daniel Smith was going to Richmond to see if he could get Mr. Clements off. I do hope he will succeed in doing so for I do hope he never will have to come in this war for it is a[n] unthankful place. I tell you I hate to see this spring campaign come on for I tell you there is going to be some hard fighting done this spring. I wish I could get in another branch of service. If I could see you all I would tell you what I is intending on doing.

Well, Ma, I close. The boys is all well except Tinsley. He is well except his leg, it is very sore yet. He was up to see me last Sunday. He said he had a[n] idea to go before the board. If he do [unclear] he will get to come home.

Nothing more at present. Still remaining your devoted son until death,

R.H. Allen

A month later, Harrison again wrote to his mother from Camp Somerville. In it he asks the family to look for a substitute to take his place.

March 26, 1864.

Dear Ma,

I avail this present opportunity this morning to inform you of my health. Dear Ma, this leaves me well at present. I hope these few lines may reach you and all the family well and doing well. Dear Ma, I would be glad to see you all though I don't know when I will see you all. I expect to get no furlough this spring so I don't know when I will get home.

Ma, I received your most kind letter. I was glad to hear from you all and hear you all was well. I haven't no news much worth writing to you at this time. Tinsley is going to start home tomorrow, so he will give you the news. I am glad he is met with the good luck to get to come home. I would give anything if I could get to come home a while.

Ma, tell Devy if he has to go to the army, tell him I don't want him to come here to this company. If I could get out of this company I would do so, but I do hope he will never have to come out in this war. I am afraid James will have to come out in this call. Ma, tell him if I was in his place, if I had to come out, I would try to go to some station battery or some cavalry if I could.

Well, Ma, as Tinsley is coming home he will give you all the news. Ma, tell Devy if he can get me a recruit and send him to me I will give him a hundred dollars. Tell him to try quickly, Page or anybody he can see. I will give a good prize; that is the only way I can get home. Ma, give all the family my best respects. Tell Ellen and Devy I would be glad to see them. Give sisters Eliza and Mary my best respects.

Your devoted son until death,

R.H. Allen

The next letter home, again from Harrison, was written from Camp Lee, near Richmond. It is unusual in that it is written on one side of the paper only, although the reverse holds two short notes.

April 2, 1864

Dear Mother,

We left Lynchburg yesterday about 5 o'clock in the morning and around about 5 o'clock p.m. [got to] Richmond. We reached our quarters about an hour after dark. A good many were afraid we might have to camp in the open air and sleep on the ground, but we were allowed to go into a large frame building and slept on bundles of straw. It is the old fair grounds where we are staying now.

I have not been to take a view of Richmond yet as we were not permitted [to go] out of camp without a written passport and of course all the boys can't get them the same day, but I intend to go down and look around soon. I would be very glad to hear from home and to see you all. If we leave here I will write soon to let you all hear where we go.

I remain your affectionate son,

Richard H. Allen

On the reverse of the above note are two paragraphs, difficult to read and apparently written in haste.

> I understand [from] Mr. Brown [since] I brought my letter to a close there will be 3 men hung on the 4th of this month in our camp. They were taken to the [unclear]. We had a great excitement this morning [rest unclear].
>
> You must excuse my scratching as there's a great deal of noises and confusion while I am writing.

Harrison wrote to his brother Devereaux, who was still at home, about two weeks later. He mentions the saltworks in Saltville, in southwestern Virginia, and expresses hope that the brigade will be transferred there, far from the current field of battle.

April 14, 1864

My dear Brother,

It is with the greatest pleasure I avail this present opportunity this morning in regard of answering your most kind letter [of] April the 10. Dear Devy, it afforded me great pleasure to hear from you and hear that you was well and doing well. Devy, this leaves me well at present. I sincerely hope when these few lines come to hand they may find you enjoying the best of health and happiness.

Dear Devy, I would be the gladdest of anything to see you at this time, but I anticipate it will be some time before I can see you all.

Devy, I haven't no news much worth your attention to write at this time, more than we are fortifying every day. We are throwing up breastworks all along on the line. They is expecting the enemy to advance on we all. I expect we will have a hard fight here before long. There is some talk of our brigade going to the salt works. I am in hopes we will go.

Well, Devy, I am glad to hear that you is getting along very well with your work, but I was very sorry to hear of John Hearse [sic] being so poorly. Poor old fellow.

Devy, tell Tinsley [that] John Broward is come to our company. Bill Crawford and him exchanged. I was going to exchange myself with John but I though it right uncertain when Tinsley would come back.

So I will change my subject. Devy, we have had a[n] abundance of rain this month. The river was full[er] last Sunday than [it has] been for many years. We had to move our picket post back from the river on account of the water.

Devy, I was sorry to hear that Daniel had to go to his company.

I must close. Give my highest regard to Ma and Ellen and Tinsley. Tell them I would be glad to see them. Tell Ma I would write to her but the boys will write to her. Give sister Eliza and Mary my best respects and Mr. Clements.

Nothing more at present. Still remain your brother until death,

R.H. Allen

Part of another letter written to Devy from Camp Somerville exists. All that remains of it is the top half of the sheet, front and back. The signature is missing, but handwriting is similar that in Richard Harrison's letters.

April 20, 1864

Dear brother Devy,

I will write you a few lines this morning in regard of my health. These few lines leave me well and able to eat all Old Jeff gives me. Our rations is very scanty. It is hard times down here with us and still getting hard[er].

Dear Devy, I do sincerely hope when these few lines come to hand they may find you and all . . .

[page torn away]

. . . my time to go over again I never would go in.

Devy, if you have to go in the army I can't tell you where to go. There is no branch of service but is hard. I think they might let you stay home for there is five of us out of one family. I think they will. If they do make you go I expect they will lose three or four men on account of it. As long as Ma has one of her sons with her I can stay in . . . [remainder missing].

On the same day, William wrote to Ellen from the 13th Virginia camp near Somerville Ford in Orange County. He offers premonitions of a big battle to come (the Wilderness) and speaks of more desertions.

April 20, 1864

Dear sister Ellen,

With great pleasure I will engage myself to my seat this morning to drop you a few lines to inform you of my health and also the times, these few lines will inform you that I am as well as for common, also all the rest of the boys are well at present. Ellen, I do sincerely hope when these few lines reach you all they may find you all in the best of health.

Ellen, I have nothing very interesting to write this morning. Times still remain awful hard and it seems like times are going to remain hard. They are still making great preparations for a fight here. It would not surprise me if it comes off at my time. It is expected to be the hardest fight that ever has been fought in Northern Virginia. It certainly will be a hard fight as there are such large forces on each side. It is said that the Yankees will have four hundred thousand to attack us. We will have a large force, though nothing to compare with the Yankee numbers. Old gen'l [James A.] Longstreet landed here a few days back. His troops was up about Charlottesville the last I heard of them. It is said that gen'l [P.G.T.] Beauregard and his force are on their way here, also gen'l Porke [sic] and his force.

We will have a large force here when all of our forces get here, it is said that we are going to cross the Rapidan and attack the Yankees. It would not surprise me at all. There is certainly a move on hand and I am afraid a very great one. I dread very much to see this fight come off because I know what we will have to undergo.

Well, Ellen, I will change my discourse. I received a letter from Daniel Burford a few days back. He was well. He is very anxious to get to this company. He wrote to me to get him a[n] exchange. I have gotten one of our company to exchange with him. I wrote on to Daniel to have his papers forwarded on. I did not insist on him at all to come to this company as I am not satisfied here myself, though he seems so anxious to get here I had to aid him. I was very much surprised to hear of him having to return back to his command.

There is a great [deal of] talk about our brigade going out [to] west Virginia to the salt works, though if we go I do not expect we will go until after this fight. I am in hopes that we will go as we have been here until I have become tired of this place.

Ellen, how are you and F. Bryan getting on? If you hear from him give him my highest regards. Ellen, tell Tinsley I wrote him a letter some time back and I never has received any answer from it at all. Ellen, James and Alexander Burks has deserted and gone to the Yankees. We was down on picket when they left. We saw James when he swam the river.

Ellen, give Ma my love and tell her I hope I will get to see her in a short time. I am in hopes the Lord may protect us in all our trials and troubles. I will have to close as we will have to go on drill.

You all must write soon and often and give us all the news. I will write again very soon. I will close, remaining your true brother till death,

William P. Allen

William was wounded in the battle of the Wilderness on May 6. He wrote to Tinsley, who was at home, from a hospital in Lynchburg.

May 10, 1864

Dear Brother Tinsley,

I will try and write you all a few lines this morning to let you all hear from me. I landed here this morning just about day[break]. Tinsley, I will inform you something about our fighting. We have certainly has had some of the hardest fighting that ever we done, though our losses are not so large owing to the fighting. We certainly did slay the Yankees, though they give it to me this time. I got shot in the thigh with a[n] Enfield ball. I has suffered a great deal, though now it is very much on the mend.

Tinsley, I want you to come over here, then I can tell you all about our [unclear]. Tinsley, I think if you or Ma was to come over here I think you all could get me off to go home. I do wish I could get to come home. Tinsley, tell Ma to come over if she can, if it would not be too much trouble to her. I have not been here long and I am sick of this place already. Tinsley, as soon as you get this letter I want you to be certain to come over.

You can tell Ma the boys was all right the last time I heard from them. I heard from them last Saturday night, though it is hard to tell how they are now. There was several of our company wounded, some one or two killed. John Crawford got killed, the same John [that] used to belong to your company. He got a[n] exchange to our company. One of the [unclear] of our company are missing [and] supposed to be killed. I don't think that many of your company got wounded. John W. Tomlinson got wounded. He is here with me. Try and [unclear].

Tinsley, try and come over. I would be glad if you would bring me some little money as I has not got a cent. We never has drawn [any pay] yet. Tinsley, if you come here, go up the Bridge Street and turn to your left on the main street. Come on down until you get near a small branch running across the street and make inquiries [for] General Hospital No. 2, Division No. 1, Ward No. 5. My ward is in the lower department of the house. The wardmaster told me he expected we would be transferred to another hospital. If you come here and we are not here, you ask him where we are transferred to. Tinsley, as soon as you get this come over. I will close remaining your true brother,

Wm. P. Allen

Harrison, Thomas and James Henry were with the 13th through the battles of the Wilderness and Spotsylvania Court House. The letter that Harrison sent to his mother a week later is written in ink on a half sheet of paper, and the uneven handwriting reflects the stress he describes.

May 19, 1864

My dear Mother,

It is with great pleasure I seat myself this morning to drop you a few lines to let you hear from me. Thanks be [to] the good Lord this leaves me well, and also Thomas and Henry. My dear Ma, I do hope these few lines may reach you all well and doing well, for I tell you it is more than I am. I has been in this war two years, but this is the [most] awful time I ever saw in my life. We has been in four hard fights. We have been in line of battle ever since the 5th of this month. We has had a hard time. There hasn't been no rest night nor day. I never saw such hard fighting in my life as we has had down here, and I am afraid the hardest fighting hasn't come off yet.

I would be so glad if the Yankees would go back across the river so we could get some rest, for I feel like I am exhausted.

Well, Ma, I reckon you heard of William getting wounded. He got quite badly wounded. Henry got a letter from him yesterday. He said he was doing very well.

Well, Ma, I will have to bring my few lines to a close as I expect [we] will have to move in a short time. The Yankees has made a move and we will have to move, too. I will write to you as soon as I can again. My chance is bad. You know how it is with me. You all must write to me. I has lost so much sleep. I am so nervous I can't write and I can't compose my mind to write this morning. But if it is the good Lord's will for me [to] live till I get in camp, I will write to you all.

But you all must write to me. Give all the family my respects, sister Eliza, and Mary, all my friends.

Please excuse this bad letter as I feel very little like writing as I did not sleep any last night.

R.H. Allen

There is a three-month break in the letters before Thomas writes to his mother from Bunker Hill in Berkeley County, north of Winchester, the base camp used by the 13th during a month of forays in the lower Valley.

August 19, 1864

Dear Mother,

As R. W. Tweedy has gotten back to his command, I thought I would write you all a few lines to let you hear from him and how he done. He went on home and stayed all the time and when he went to start back he went to the enrollment officer and the enrollment officer give him a passport or something of that kind and wrote to the provost in Lynchburg to give him a passport so that is all the papers he gotten to show when he came back. So he is all right and Henry, you had better see the enrollment officer and get some show to bring with you.

You may do as you please, but I would come as soon as I could get back. The Col. is taken all of your names and is going to send them to the enrollment officer to arrest all he can see and send them here under guard. Tell Henry [that] Tweedy says if he can't get transportation from the enrollment officer he would report to Staunton. He told Lt. Stringfellow. He saw him in Lexington, so he thinks he is at the hospital. [unclear] If I thought you could get transportation from the enrollment officer of the county, I would do so without fail, though I reckon he will be there before this gets there.

We left Winchester this morning and have marched here at Bunkers Hill. I like [it] out here. My health is splendid. I enjoy myself in eating. My duty is light. I stay with the doctor so I don't have anything to do. If I had, I would of played out before this time. Well, I must close. I don't reckon you can hardly read this. I wrote it walking along the road.

T.O. Allen

A month later, James wrote the letter that no mother wants to read from camp near Strasburg, Virginia, in the Shenandoah Valley. The 13th had participated in the battle of Winchester on the day before.

September 20, 1864

Dear Mother,

With a sad heart I take pen in hand to drop you a few lines
to let you all hear from me. These few lines leave me just only
tolerable. Well, Ma, I sincerely hope when these few lines
come to hand they find you and all of the family well and doing
well. Dear Mother, we had a[n] awful battle yesterday. We
fought from daylight until dark. Ma, I am sorry to have to tell
you that poor Harrison got mortally wounded. He was
wounded in the head. The ball went in about the top of his
[unclear]. It cut his head wide open. Thomas and Bob Tweedy
carried him off to the hospital at Winchester. Tom Lloyd, he
did not think he would live to see this morning.

Thomas said he would talk to him and he never give him
no answer. He said he even never winked his eyes all the time
he was with him. Tom told the doctor to attend to him well,
and the doctor told him he would. Poor fellow. He is left in
the hands of the enemy.

We had to fall back. The Yankees was too hard for us. We
lost a great deal of men yesterday. We had 18 in our company
and now we ain't got [but] about 5 of them is killed and 6
wounded.

Dear Mother, me and Thomas came out safe, only Tom, he
got slightly struck on the shoulder but it did not break the skin.
Our colonel [George A.] Goodman was killed dead. We don't
have no colonel now.

Well, Ma, as I have given you all the news I will bring my
few lines to close. Give sister Mary and her family my best
respects and also Mr. Clements and sister and family my best
respects and tell them to write and give me all the news. So,
nothing more, only I remain your true son until death,

James H. Allen

P.S. You must excuse me for my bad writing and spelling as I am in much of a hurry. Write soon, Ma, and give me all the news. Haven't received but one since I left home. This is my 3 only. [?]

Four days later, Thomas also wrote to his mother of Harrison's death. He and Henry had become separated, and Thomas thought that Henry had been wounded and/or captured. He had not.

September 24, 1864

Dear Mother,

I sadly seat myself this Saturday morning to try and pen you a few lines to inform you of my health. I am happy to say to you this leaves me quite well in body but troubled in mind.

I reckon you have heard of brother Harrison getting so badly wounded. He was wounded in the head. I carried him to Winchester. The Yankees pressed us so hard we had to leave in a very short time after getting there with him. That was on the 19th of this month and on the 22 of this month we all had to run again, so I has not seen Henry since. I heard he is wounded. I am almost sure the Yankees have gotten him and my captain, too.

Lots of our men is gone and we don't know how they went, though they are missing and that's all we know. We run about three miles each day, so they have gotten all of our wounded both days and all that could not run fast. I tell you, Ma, I almost flew. Some went to the mountains so I hear. Henry may be with them. They were scattered worse there.

I heard that poor Harrison did not speak after he was struck. I tell you we here lost [an] awful chance of men this last week, though I know all of them was not killed. I has gotten Harrison's money. I wish you would let me know what to do with it. I could send it to you in a letter but it might get misplaced, so I will do as you say. I can't say how much he has for I have not looked.

I am bound to close at it is raining and I am on picket at this time.

My dear Mother, you must excuse my short letter as it is raining so I can't write any more at this time. I still remain yours truly until death,

T. O. Allen

James wrote to Ellen from the camp at New Market a month later.

October 25, 1864

Dear sister Ellen,

Thanks be to the Lord I am spared to write you all a few more lines again. Ellen, these few lines leave me well and hearty as ever. I do sincerely hope when these few lines come to hand they may find you and all the family well.

Dear Ellen, we had another hard battle on the 19th inst. at Newtown. We whipped the Yankees in the morning and captured a great many wagons and artillery and most everything they had, and in the even[ing] they charged us and broke our line of battle and got our men stampeded and they retaken everything back and a great deal besides.

Our forces had to fall back to New Market. A great many of our men had to take to the mountains. I did myself, although I wasn't but 2 or 3 days in the mountains before I got to my company. There is several hasn't come in yet.

Dear Ellen, it seems like we have very bad luck out here in the Valley. The Yankees has too many men for us.

Ellen, it looks like it is no use of me writing to you all for I can't get no answer from you all. I have wrote 4 or 5 letters to you all and I haven't got but [one] letter since I have left you all. I can't tell whether you all get mine or not, but I would be more than glad to [be] receiving a letter from you all.

Ellen, I want you to write to give me all the news and write to me all about the boys. I can't hear a word about them. You can tell William if he is at home that our company is quite small. We have no officers, not even a sergeant. We are just here with no one to [unclear] at all.

Dear Ellen, give sister Mary Whitten and family my best

respects and also sister Eliza and Mr. Clements and family and
tell them to write and tell me how they [are] getting on.

Ellen, I would give most anything to see you all. I am in
hopes this cruel war will soon be over. I can get home to stay
in. I don't think I can stay in no longer and this year no how.

Well, Ellen, will have to close my few badly written lines so
I will remain your true brother until death,

James H. Allen

A letter to Eliza Allen Clements on November 3 from New Market has
some pieces torn away. The handwriting appears to be that of James.

November 3, 1864

Dear sister Eliza,

It is with the greatest pleasure I do seat myself this morning
to write you [missing] in regards of my health [missing]. These
few lines leave me as well as for common. Dear sister, I do
sincerely hope when those few lines come to hand they may
find you and your family enjoying good health. Dear sister, I
would be more than glad to see you and family.

I am in hopes I will get a furlough this winter so that I can
pay you all one more visit. They all says that all of the
sharpshooters will get a few days furlough this winter. If I do
get it I am in hopes I can enjoy several good hours with you
all. I wish I was at your house with [missing] for I think you
can put up a better breakfast than I had. All I get is a small
hoecake of bread and about a half pound of beef for my day's
ration. We get about half rations at the present, but we have
had very rough times out here.

Since I left home we have had hard fighting and marching.
The morning we went around to flank the Yankees I thought
I would almost freeze. We had to ford the Shenandoah River
about daylight. I was just as wet as a rat, and we went right on
into the fight without seeing a spark of fire, and that night I
had to pitch right into the river again or be captured, one or
the other. I tell you, the soldiers sees hard times.

Dear sister, I do hope and pray this awful war will soon [missing]. I don't see nor hear no talk of it ending soon. Way they is taking out all the [unclear] men it don't look much like peace.

Sister, Mr. Sandridge and Ned Crawford and Henry Dani— [missing].

Sister, I would like to know what is Mr. Clements going to do or what he is doing. Sister, I know if Mr. Clements has to leave you I know there is no place for you to be. I do hope and trust in the Lord [that] he won't have to come in the army, for I do not think it is right to take him from you. [section missing] I am thinking starvation will be the ending of this war yet.

Sister, I want you to answer this letter as soon as it comes to hand. I can't tell what is the reason I don't get [letters] from home. I can't hear a word from home. I can't tell whether they get my letters or not. I would be more than glad to hear from [them].

Well, sister, I will bring my few lines to close. If Mr. Clements is at home, give him my best respects and tell him to write to me and give me all the [rest of letter missing].

As the war wound on, even Devereaux, the youngest son, left the family farm in Amherst and went into service. He wrote to his mother from Camp Staunton Bridge, the final letter of 1864.

December 19, 1864

Dear Mother,

It is with much pleasure that I embrace the present opportunity of writing you a few lines to let you know where and how I am after a long silence. We are not at the same place we were when I last wrote to you. I have never received a single letter from home since I have been here, which is now better than a month. I got a letter from Tinsley since I have been here. He was in Lynchburg. He told me not to write to him any more until I heard from him again. We received orders the other day to go into North Carolina. We started on the 9th of the month and went down to Kinston, N.C., to meet the Vandr— raiders, but they started the day before we got there. We pursued the next day but failed to overtake them. We then came back to town and returned to this place. We suffered very much with cold in one journey. We were on the road for about eight days. We met with several accidents on the cars, but none of us got hurt. We also suffered for something to eat for we had no [unclear] cook on [unclear].

All of the boys are well and [unclear]. I would like to get home for Christmas but cannot do so. You must write to me as soon as you get this and give me all the news from home. Give my love to all at home and believe me to be your affectionate son,

D. F. Allen

1865

The first letter of 1865 was written by Tinsley to his mother from the College Hospital in Lynchburg.

My Dear Ma,

I embrace this my earliest opportunity of answering your kind letter of the 8th [unclear] to hand this morning which gives me great pleasure to hear that all was well and that you met with the luck to get a hand to attend to your outward business.

Dear Ma, I have nothing of importance to communicate. Times is quite dull at this place. It is the general impression that Virginia will be evacuated this coming spring. Everything is at a tremendous price. Cornbread is worth two dollars per lb., flour from five to six hundred dollars per barrel. I purchased cloth enough for cart pants and trimming, [for] which I give the rise of seven hundred dollars and by the time they are made they will cost me the rise of nine hundred dollars. It is not worth a man's while to talk dressing now unless he is a speculator. I haven't had my coat made yet. I thought cloth was getting higher daily. I can have it made at any time.

Dear Ma, I did expect you would of been over at the city before this time. I sent the things you was speaking of. I written in my last letter about the trip we had to Wytheville in pursuit of the Yankees. I had a very good time of it. People was very kind in that portion of the country.

My ink is so skim I fear that it will be hard for you to read the letter. I hadn't heard anything from home since I left until the arrival of this letter. I was very glad to hear from you all once more. Give my regards to all friends. May these few lines reach you and all enjoying the sweet blessings of this life. Ma, I am, as usual, still remaining your devoted son until death,

                                                                    T. L. A.

Ten days later, Tinsley wrote to his mother from Camp Gordon in Dinwiddie County, Virginia, where he had rejoined his regiment.

                                                                    January 22, 1865

Dear Ma,

I now avail myself the opportunity of dropping you a few lines to inform you of my destination. I reached my command the 19th, finding all well. I am with Thomas today. He is well and doing well. We have good quarters, I believe the best since the war started. He and Lockwood is together. Lockwood sends his highest regards. He and Thomas is doing well.

Is William and Henry give out the idea going = = = [sic] I haven't heard from them since I left home.

We are about 9 miles on the east side of Petersburg, about 3 miles off the railroad. I have no news of importance to communicate more than things have advanced very much since the [unclear] of Fort Fisher. Things are going very fast. I do not know [if] we will live if there is no change and fear there will be none for the better. It's enough to give us all a sad heart to contemplate. I haven't reported for duty yet and I don't know whether I will soon.

I reached here today. I left Lynchburg, Capt. [Hugh Nelson] Burks and all of the company are well. He appeared like he was very glad to see me. He said he had a very dull Christmas. I would [have] gotten him a dram if it had not been so high in Lynchburg. I had a fine eggnog the night before I left Lynchburg with my little lady love. I stayed at her Ma's the night before I started. For the first time I enjoyed myself very much, making a great many manifestations, now more than I expect to comply with. I hope I shall see her soon.

I will write soon again. Give my highest regards to all [unclear] friends. This leaves me well [unclear] to my jaw. I had two teeth extracted the day before I left. May these few lines reach you enjoying the sweet blessings of this life.

Still remaining your devoted son until death,

T. L. A.

James Clements, too, finally entered the service, in the 51st Virginia. He wrote this letter to his wife, Eliza, from Camp Lee, near Richmond, Virginia.

March 15, 1865

My dear Wife,

I seat myself this evening to let you know how I am getting along. I am well at present and I hope these few lines may find you and all the family well. I have had a very bad cold. I am nearly well of that.

I am still at Camp Lee yet. I do not know how long I will stay here. I cannot hear from the regiment where I wanted to go to. I chose the 51st regiment and Captain Henley's company.

My duty is very light at this time. There is 6 of us to guard the women from selling whiskey. We captured 83 bottles this morning.

I think there is a fight close to hand here. We was ordered out to the ditches last Sunday and we stayed out 2 days.

My dear, you must not think too much about me. I am in a very good house. I has never suffered for anything to eat as yet. If you can hear where Capt. Henley's company is, send word of him. [I have] seen a great many men here, but have not seen but one that I knew. That was Nat Higginbotham. I want you to write all up there about the boys. You must write the news as soon as you get this letter. I would like better to hear from you than to hear any other news I could hear except permission to go home. Try and make some corn in if you can. Give my love to Ma and Mary [unclear] and kiss the children for me. I could write something more but my eyes get so full I cannot see how to write.

Write word how to direct letters to the boys so I can write to them. You can direct your letters to Camp Lee, Va. I hope to [rest of paragraph smudged and unclear].

Your devoted husband until death,

James Clements

William wrote to his mother from Camp Petersburg, Virginia, near the Union's Fort Stedman. He mentions their cabins, called shebangs, which were dug underground and reinforced with timbers. Although small, some of them were fixed up with fireplaces and shelves for storage. Morale was low, desertion high.

March 17, 1865

Dear Ma,

I have once more seated myself to drop you a few lines to let you hear from me and also to let you hear where we are. I am quite well at this time, though our fare is very common, our rations are very short. I do hope when these few lines come to hand they may find you all enjoying the greatest of health. I would be more than glad to hear from home at this time. I have not heard one word from you all since I had been down here and it seems like we will not hear from there again soon.

I cannot hear whether the Yankees came through to give you all a call or not, though I am in hopes they did not. If I could hear from you all I would be much better satisfied. We never has been kept in as much darkness since this war has been going on, though there will be nothing gained by that.

I have a great deal of news to write which I would write if I thought you would get the mail, though it is very uncertain about you all getting the mail. There has not been the first letter received from Amherst since I has been down here.

Thomas has not received a letter from Beck since I came down. The mail train has not been running regular to Lynchburg. I have written several letters up to Lynchburg, one or two to Daniel Burford and I have not had from one of them, though I am looking every day for one.

Ma, I will tell you something about our camp. We has moved about ten miles. We are now right at Petersburg. Our regiment are right on [the] Appomattox River. Our cabins are about ten steps from the river. We have been in a great many quarters, though these bang out any I has seen.

We are in a fort breastworks and it is one of the most confining places that ever I was in. We cannot hold our heads over the breastworks. We [have] steady firing on the line day and night. We are about fifty yards from each other. The Yankees could take this city all to pieces if they would. We are compelled to have awful hard fighting on this line, and we are expecting for the fight to come off at any time. I dread to see it take place.

Our men are deserting awful bad at this time. Before we moved down here our brigade deserted awfully. Three from Capt. Burks's deserted night before last. James M. Staton, Cliff Staton and Sim Staton all went to the Yankees, and there was several more went the same night. There was four more started and they were caught and brought back. They will be sentenced to be shot.

Ma, if Tinsley is at home, give him my highest regards and tell him I reckon his regiment will be broke up. All of the officers went before an examination board and every one of them was thrown over. Round Charles Henderson was thrown over. He talks of going to Mosby's cavalry. I will tell you that [the] company is awfully dissatisfied.

Ma, I forgot to tell you about our cabins. They are entirely underground, just long enough for about four to stay in. Me and Tom and Lockwood and Ormond Tomlin and our lieutenant [Hugh P. Powell] are in one mess.

Ma, I will tell you all those who are caught and brought in

here. After this I do believe [they] will be shot. I can venture to say if any of the Coffey's are caught they will be shot. I never want to see them brought back here. This is a hard life to live and it is hard to stay at home, though if I were at home I expect I would try and stay.

I would be better satisfied if I could hear from home. They are certain something going on that I do not like as we could hear from home.

Ma, I have not heard from Jimmy since I left him for Richmond. Ma, if Devy is at home yet, give him my love and tell Henry to be certain to write and give me all the news. I will close with my love.

Remaining with you all, nothing more than remaining your true son until death,

Wm. T. Allen

William wrote to Henry from Camp Petersburg a week later, the day before the disastrous Confederate assault on Fort Stedman.

March 24, 1865

Henry,

I have seated myself this morning to drop you and the family a few lines to let you all to know I am getting along. I am as well as you might expect at this time, though for a few days back I was very unwell, though I think it was by exposure. We have a great deal of duty to do at this place and the weather has been very inclement. I do hope when these few lines reach you and the family they may find you all enjoying the best of health.

Henry, I would be more than glad to hear from you all. Since I left home I has written Ma two letters though I cannot tell if she has gotten them or not though I am in hopes that she has. When I write I hardly know where to direct my letters to as our mail has been so confused. I directed the last one to the Buffalo Springs to the care of Mr. W. White, as I cannot tell whether there is any mail to New Glasgow or not.

Henry, will give you a sketch about our army. We are tolerable quiet at this time, though I will tell you it has been very unpleasant here. There has been a continuous fire on the line with musketry. There has been several of our men wounded and some killed. One was shot dead in our yard [the] day before yesterday.

I have been in service for some time, though this place bangs out any that ever I was in. Our shebangs are some ten or fifteen feet under the earth, though some of us have small cabins that are not under the earth that we can stay in when they are not shelling. We have the greatest breastworks here that I ever has seen. We are expecting a[n] awful fight on our lines every day, and they will be sure to fight in a short time. They cannot stage two large armies this close together and not fight. This is one of the most confining places that I ever I was. We cannot show our heads to a Yankee unless he fires at us.

We are permitted to visit Petersburg on a pass, though there is no use in our visiting of that place. All of our men are entirely out of money and everything is so awful high. There is talk of our drawing money soon, though I think it doubtful.

Henry, our brigades are going to be consolidated. They are going to put the 49th with our regiment and they are going to put the 58th & 52nd & 31st all together and only have two regiments out of the whole. All of our officers went before a[n] examination and I will tell you that there was a great many was throwed overboard. Nearly every one in the 58th was throwed over. Capt. Burks's company will go up. Charley Henderson is going to resign as he cannot hold his office. I will tell you there is a great confusion in that company. And not only in that company, it is all through the whole brigade.

We have the choice to go to any company in the brigade that we want to go to. I expect Lt. Stringfellow will be our captain and Lt. Powell will stand. Our captain will be throwed over, also Maj. Critton. I [would] tell you who the officers will be, though it is too tedious to mention.

I will change my subject. Henry, I will remark a few things

to you.

Every man who is caught now and brought back here, I would not give two cents for his life. And again there are a certain person that are going to do everything to get them all caught that he [can]. Oh, I will tell you he is red hot for them. I do pray that I never may see one of the Coffeys brought back here. If I was at home now I know I would keep out of their way. I do believe that every man in the mountains are coming home the first chance. I cannot tell how many has been after me to come with them.

I will tell you that I am not satisfied here by no means. This is one trying place. Our rations are awful short. There is some talk about our camps going back to the valley. The Yankees are mining down here and our men are also. I reckon we will have a great blow down here in a few days. I do trust and pray that this war will come to a close in a few days.

Henry, when you write I want you to write me a long letter and give me the news about everything. Let me know what all of the mountain boys are doing.

Henry, if you hear from James Clements, let me know. I am afraid he will come to this company. Our [unclear] are going to be a[n] awful tight company.

Henry, let me hear where Tinsley is and also Devy. I heard that Devy had come home on furlough, and I heard he had joined the station battery at Richmond.

Henry, give Ma and Ellen my love and tell them I would like to see them. Also give sister Eliza & Mary my love also and tell them they must be sure to write to me. Henry, tell Ellen & Ma that I will write very soon to them again.

Thomas is quite well and all the rest of the neighborhood boys. Henry, you must be sure to write as soon as you get this letter and give me the points about everything. I will have to close as my paper is about to give out. I will close still remaining your true and devoted absent brother until death departs us,

Wm. T. Allen

P.S. Henry, tell Tinsley that his papers was sent back from Richmond, though they was not approved. They was put in wrong. His papers call for the first lieutenant and they sent them back saying that there was no first lieutenant registered there, though you can tell him they was put in and sent back again.

On the same day, Thomas wrote to his wife from the same camp. Two days later, before it could be mailed, he added the sad news of William's death.

March 24, 1865

Dear Wife,

I seat myself this Friday evening to pen you a few lines to let you hear from me. This leaves me quite well and doing well and I hope this may find you enjoying the same good blessings. Dear Wife, I don't have much news to write to you at [this] time for I can't hear from you so I can't have much to write. Have not heard from you but once since the Yankee raid. I was glad that they did not get there with you all. I received the letters that you wrote on the 13 & 14. You put both in one envelope. That is the only one I have received from you since the 2 day of March. So you may know I don't hear from you often though I can't think it is your fault, yet I write to you as often as I have done heretofore and I hope you will do so too. I would as soon to be at Washington City as to be here and can't hear from you, for that is all the pleasure I have is to hear from you. So I hope you will write soon and often. If my letters cannot get to you I am sorry, though I think they ought to go without any difficulty.

I will say to you we are here in less than a mile of Petersburg. I am in full view of the city and I like [it] very well. I make out tolerable well. I have a good house.

Will is here, and Mr. Clements went on to Richmond so I have not heard from him since, and Henry did not come no further than Amherst C.H., so I reckon he is at home, though I don't know where he is. I reckon Tinsley is at home by this time.

I hope you will write soon and let me hear all of the news.

I will say to you one of my regiment got shot this week. He was shot by a Yankee. He was shot [with]in a [few] feet of my door. We shoot at each other all the time. He lived about 3 hours after he was shot. I ran out and took him to the doctor, but his time had come so he was bound to die.

I like [it] very well. I hope we may stay here sometime for I don't think we will have much fighting to do here.

My Dear, I want to say to you one thing, that is if I ever do get so I can't hear from you, I hope you will not be uneasy about me, for I expect if [unclear] it will be so some time or another. So you must not never be distressed about me, no way, no shape. I will get there some time or other, though if my home was given up I do think I would be sure to come there. Let things be as they might be, though I believe when my home is given up the war will be at a close.

Some thinks Ole Virginia will be given up, though I don't. I hear some talk of our corps going to the Valley. I can't say where we are going. Myself, I would as soon believe we will stay here as any other way.

Well, I believe I will close for this time as I expect to write soon again, though I hope I will have the good luck of hearing from you before I write again. So I will close by saying I still remain your true and loving husband until death parts us,

Thomas O. Allen

The second letter is scratched below the first. The handwriting reflects the haste and the words carry the emotion of the severe losses when the Confederates attacked Fort Stedman on March 25. The southerners breached the Union lines but were repulsed, losing 4,000 men, many of them taken prisoner. Union losses were fewer than 1,500.

Dear Wife,

With a sad heart I seat myself this Sunday morning to pen you a few lines to let you know that I am well in body but troubled in my mind.

Oh, my Dear, I reckon you have heard of the big fight that was on the 25th. Oh, my Dear, it awful time with [unclear] before soldiers to charge such breastworks. Oh, my Dear, you can't tell my feeling.

This morning my Dear Brother William was killed dead and several good friends. Lt. Powell was killed dead. I saw both of them buried last night. Lockheart [sic] came out safe. I tell you it was [an] awful hot place though we took their works but could not hold them. Our loss was pretty heavy. I know 8 of my regiment was killed dead and I can't say how many more and [unclear] wounded and [unclear] prisoners. It was a wise man that was taken prisoner that day. I believe if I ever get in another such place I'll go up. Don't you think? So a man had better go up as to be killed.

Yours truly,

T. O. A.

"Going up" was a euphemism for surrendering. A few days later Thomas again took pen to hand, this time to let Sallie know of the family's great loss of a second brother.

March 30, 1865

Dear sister Sallie,

With a sad heart I seat myself this morning to pen you a few lines to inform you of my health. This leaves me quite well in body but troubled in mind.

Dear Sister, I reckon you have heard of the fight that was fought on the 25 inst. Oh, my dear sister, I reckon you have heard of brother William's getting killed. He was killed dead, but I hope he is better off. He was shot through his body. He was dead when I first saw him. I am glad to say he was very attentive to his testament since he came down. Oh, I hope he is better off than he was here, for I tell you there is no pleasure to be seen here, such times as there are now.

Lt. Powell was killed dead also and [unclear] Dempsey also. Our loss was heavy. We charged the Yankee's breastworks and took them, but could not hold them. It was [an] awful time with we all. The Yankees charged our works last night, twice, but could not get them. We drove them back both times. Our loss was small.

Oh, I am so sorry for my dear mother. It is so hard on her, though you must talk to her and cheer her up all you can. I will say to you that William was buried very nice considering [the] way the times was. He was buried in a coffin about half a mile from Petersburg. I had him put away as well as I could. I sent his things up yesterday that I could get by express. I sent a box up to John Howl[sic] and put his things in it. So if you see Mother, you can tell her I wrote to her day before yesterday. I hope she will get it, though I reckon it is uncertain about her getting of it.

I have not heard of James Clements since William came down. I received a letter from Daniel Burford [the] day before yesterday that he had written to William. I would of answered it, though I did not know how to direct it so I did not write. Lots of our boys is going home and to the Yankees all the time. I will say to you if I get in many more hard places I expect to be a prisoner myself, for I can't risk myself as I have done. So if I am missing at any time, I hope you all will not be uneasy about me.

I heard from my dear wife a few days ago. She was well. Dear Sister, I hope this cruel war will soon end, as I believe it will.

Well, I must bring my few lines to a close as I was up fighting all last night and it is raining and dark so as I can't hardly see how to write. Excuse bad writing [unclear] as I don't feel like writing.

So I will close by saying I ever remain your true and loving brother until death.

T. O. Allen

After the War

Four of the boys returned home after Appomattox: Tinsley, James Henry, Thomas and Devereaux.

A memorial service was held for William and Richard Harrison at the family's church, Mt. Horeb Methodist in Amherst County, on November 4, 1866. The minister used verses 24 and 25 of the first chapter of Peter. He declared,

> I am requested by the friends and associates to hold a remembrance service for William and Richard Allen whose recent deaths have brought sadness to the hearts of so many relatives and friends. It is still more solemn when we remember that they have met the fate of so many thousands who fell victims to death in the last four or five years which has clothed our entire county inhabitants in war and made it a valley of weeping. Perhaps there is not one in the congregation who does not feel sad because of some friends who have fallen like the two we commend today.

Tinsley, the eldest brother, became a leading citizen of Amherst C.H. He was vice president of the Bank of Amherst and a merchant there. He died in 1909 at age 78, and the *Amherst New Era Progress* ran this eulogy on April 25:

For forty years a succesful merchant of Amherst where he had large and growing affairs under his control, his life was an open book, known and read by all men, and if an honest man is the noblest work of God, then was he as noble a [unclear] as ever lived. Honest not only where dollars were involved, but honest in his opinions of [unclear]. Too honest ever to appear or make believe that he was [unclear] he had opinions different from what the sincerity of his nature told him was right. And this high sense of honor produced singular independence of thought and action that at times made him appear aloof from his fellowmen, but it was all on the surface; he had never learned how to [unclear] his convictions of what he considered right.

His independence of character and his absolute dependence upon God at once furnished the touchstone of his life. He possessed a simple faith and trust in God and the Bible that was the admiration and joy of the spiritually minded. His knowledge of the scriptures was profound and inspiring and truly he had reached that point where he loved righteousness for righteousness's sake.

As a father and husband he taught peace, reverence for the truth, love, charity, fairness, tenderness; that there is not lasting happiness that is not founded upon the noblest [unclear] of God's nature.

Thomas, who was married before the war began, was a storekeeper in the area. Henry moved to West Virginia and remained the bachelor of the family. Devereaux, the youngest, returned to his home. He was so young that he stayed with Dr. Smith, a medical doctor, and attended a private school called Oldwood. He married D. Lane, ran a small store on the place and farmed, raising corn, wheat and tobacco.

A communion table for the Mt. Horeb Methodist church was dedicated to the Allen family in 1965. It was crafted by Sam Burford of Monroe from walnut found on the Allen place.

Index